**INSTRUCTOR'S RESOURCE MANUAL
WITH TEST BANK FOR**

THEORY AND PRACTICE OF GROUP COUNSELING

Fifth Edition

Gerald Corey
California State University at Fullerton

Australia • Canada • Denmark • Japan • Mexico • New Zealand • Philippines
Puerto Rico • Singapore • South Africa • Spain • United Kingdom • United States

COPYRIGHT (c) 2000 Wadsworth.
Brooks/Cole Counseling is an imprint of Wadsworth, a division of Thomson Learning. Thomson Learning is a trademark used herein under license.

All Rights Reserved. No part of this work may be reproduced, transcribed or used in any form or by any means—graphic, electronic, or mechanical, including photocopying, recording, taping, web distribution or information storage and retrieval systems—without the written permission of the publisher.

Printed in Canada
1 2 3 4 5 6 7 03 02 01 00 99

For permission to use material from this text,
contact us by
    Web: www.thomsonrights.com
    Fax: 1-800-730-2215
    Phone: 1-800-730-2214

ISBN 0-534-36647-3

For more information, contact
Wadsworth/Thomson Learning
10 Davis Drive
Belmont, CA 94002-3098
USA
www.wadsworth.com

International Headquarters
Thomson Learning
290 Harbor Drive, 2nd Floor
Stamford, CT 06902-7477
USA

UK/Europe/Middle East
Thomson Learning
Berkshire House
168-173 High Holborn
London WC1V 7AA
United Kingdom

Asia
Thomson Learning
60 Albert Complex
Singapore 189969

Canada
Nelson/Thomson Learning
1120 Birchmount Road
Scarborough, Ontario M1K 5G4
Canada

CONTENTS

Part I	Some Suggestions for Teaching Courses in Group Counseling	1
Part II	Perspectives and Practices on the Education and Training of Group Leaders	23
Part III	Guidelines and Suggestions for Chapters	36

Learning Objectives, Key Terms, Lecture Outlines, Focus Questions, T-F and Multiple-Choice Quizzes

Chapter 1	Introduction to Group Work	39
Chapter 2	Group Leadership	41
Chapter 3	Ethical and Professional Issues in Group Practice	48
Chapter 4	Early Stages in the Development of a Group	51
Chapter 5	Later Stages in the Development of a Group	57
	Unit Test on the Basic Elements of Group Process: An Overview	61
Chapter 6	The Psychoanalytic Approach to Groups	67
Chapter 7	Adlerian Group Counseling	77
Chapter 8	Psychodrama	84
Chapter 9	The Existential Approach to Groups	92
Chapter 10	The Person-Centered Approach to Groups	98
Chapter 11	Gestalt Therapy	104
Chapter 12	Transactional Analysis	110

Chapter 13	Behavioral Group Therapy	116
Chapter 14	Rational Emotive Behavior Therapy in Groups	123
Chapter 15	Reality Therapy in Groups	131
Chapter 16	Comparisons, Contrasts, and Integration	139
Chapter 17	The Evolution of a Group: An Integrative Perspective	140

Part IV   Guidelines for Study and Preparation:
Final Examination — 141
Take Home Practice Final Examination — 143

Part V   Final Examination for Theory and Practice of Group Counseling — 161

Appendix I: Answer Key to Final Examination — 195

Appendix II: InfoTrac Flow Chart — 196

PREFACE

In this *Instructor's Manual with Test Items,* which is designed to accompany both *Theory and Practice of Group Counseling, Fifth Edition,* and the *Student Manual for Theory and Practice of Group Counseling, Fifth Edition,* my aim is to share with you ideas that I've found useful in teaching my own courses in group counseling at the undergraduate and graduate levels. In this manual, I present many ideas and suggestions concerning the content and structure of the group counseling course, and I share the experiences and problems I've had in this course. I offer questions, exercises, activities, learning objectives, lecture outlines and notes, objective test items, discussion and essay examination questions, and suggestions for a format for teaching group counseling courses, including both didactic *and* experiential components. Another aim is to discuss some of the problems and issues that I cncounter in the teaching, training, and supervising of group counselors: grading, consultation, training approaches, basic ethical and professional issues in training and supervising group leaders, methods of teaching self-evaluation, and methods of evaluating and giving feedback to groups.

I've prepared this manual as a springboard for you to develop your own ideas about and approaches to teaching your group courses. I am *not* attempting to push one way of teaching such courses, but merely presenting material that I find valuable. Each of you, whether a beginning or advanced and experienced instructor, will have your own ideas that fit your personal style of teaching and will meet the unique needs of the students you teach. There is more material in this manual (and the combination of the textbook and the *Student Manual*) than can be fully covered in one semester. My hope is that you'll take whatever you find useful and modify and expand the material to suit your teaching style and your situation.

I'd be very interested in hearing from you regarding ways that you teach your courses or special materials that you've developed for them. Also, I'd like to know how you and your students use both the textbook and this manual. I welcome any reactions you'd care to share with me. Please communicate with me directly by writing to my home address: P.O. Box 2038, Idyllwild, California 92549. My home phone number is (909) 659-4320. You can fax me at (909) 659-6117. My e-mail is cordileone@aol.com.

Gerald Corey

PART I
Some Suggestions for Teaching Courses
in Group Counseling

PART I
Some Suggestions for Teaching Courses in Group Counseling

In this section I'd like to share some approaches I have used in teaching the group counseling courses, both in undergraduate and graduate programs. I offer these materials and guidelines for you to consider as you prepare your own courses. Again, I encourage you to use whatever appeals to you or those ideas that you think you'd like to try. Sharing these ideas and experiences are aimed at generating your own adaptations of teaching approaches and techniques.

1. The core textbook is *Theory and Practice of Group Counseling* (5th ed.). To add to the experiential emphasis in the course, the *Manual for Theory and Practice of Group Counseling* (5th ed.) can also be used. I developed this manual through materials that I gave in class; thus, most of the material in the manual has been class tested.

2. For reading suggestions, I refer students to the list of books in the textbook after Part I (Chapters 1–5: see pages 136–142) and at the end of each of the separate theory chapters in Part II (Chapters 6–15).

3. Some specific books that you may find useful in preparing for your classes are:

   a. Brabender, V., & Fallon, A. (1993). *Models of inpatient group psychotherapy*. Washington, D.C.: American Psychological Association.

   b. Donigan, J., & Hulse-Killacky, D. (1999). *Critical incidents in group therapy* (2nd ed.). Pacific Grove, CA: Brooks/Cole.

   c. Donigan, J., & Malnati, R. (1997). *Systemic group therapy*. Pacific Grove, CA: Brooks/Cole.

   d. Gladding, S. T. (1991). *Group work: A counseling specialty*. New York: Merrill.

   e. Jacobs, E. E., Masson, R. L., & Harvill, R. L. (1998). *Group counseling: Strategies and skills* (3rd ed.). Pacific Grove, CA: Brooks/Cole.

   f. Shapiro, J. L., Pelz, L. S., & Bernadett-Shapiro, S. (1998). *Brief group treatment: Practical training for therapists and counselors*. Pacific Grove, CA: Brooks/Cole.

   g. Yalom, I. (1995). *The theory and practice of group psychotherapy* (4th ed.). New York: Basic Books.

   h. Yalom, I. D. (1983). *Inpatient group psychotherapy*. New York: Basic Books.

4. Other books, workbooks, and videos in the group field which my colleagues and I have developed and published with Brooks/Cole are:

   a. Corey, G., Corey, M., & Haynes, R. (2000). *Student workbook to accompany student video: Evolution of a group.* Pacific Grove, CA: Brooks/Cole · Wadsworth.

   b. Corey, G., & Corey, M. (1997). *I never knew I had a choice* (6th ed.). Pacific Grove, CA: Brooks/Cole.

   c. Corey, G., Corey, M., Callanan, P., & Russell, J. M. (1992*). Group techniques* (2nd ed.). Pacific Grove, CA: Brooks/Cole.

   d. Corey, M., & Corey, G. (1997). *Groups: Process and practice* (5th ed.). Pacific Grove, CA: Brooks/Cole.

5. Our classes meet in three-hour blocks once a week, or twice each week for 75 minutes each session. During this time, I devote the first half of the session to lecturing or presenting new ideas in addition to the materials in the chapters. The second half of the session is devoted to small group discussions or whole-class discussion (see the questions in this resource manual after each chapter for common questions for these discussions), or for demonstration of certain group techniques. In addition to these weekly three-hour meetings, I typically schedule a weekend workshop early in the semester off campus. The nature and structure of these weekend training workshops are described in detail later in this manual. My colleagues and I have also experimented with conducting a graduate group course using a format of an intensive weeklong experience. It is imperative that the students complete the required reading prior to the weeklong intensive, and we also schedule a follow-up meeting as a group if it is practical. The students have papers due some time after the experience of the week. During the semester, students write several take-home position papers dealing with the content in the textbooks. During the final examination week we meet for a wrap-up session, which is followed by an objective-type final examination.

6. In this *Instructor's Manual,* you'll find chapter quizzes (both true-false and multiple-choice items for each of the theory chapters) along with focus questions (which can be used for in-class or take-home quizzes/exams) and a final examination on the various theories. The questions on the final examination can be used as a partial basis for determining the course grade. The chapter quizzes are utilized not so much for grading as they are for students to check their progress. The students use the chapter tests and quizzes as self-check devices, along with the comprehension checks in the *Student Manual.*

7. Student evaluations of the course and instructor can be of real value, especially if they are given at some middle point during the semester, and not just at the end of the course. Generally, I give two types of student evaluations that I have designed (in addition to the required

brief evaluation required by the department). One is a short-essay type of student evaluation that I give before the midterm; the other is an objective-type of questionnaire that I use toward the end of the course.

8. Another source for evaluations of the various aspects of the course is the conference with a student. I encourage students to come in during office times to discuss their field placements and other aspects of the course. I've found it valuable to have two students (who co-lead groups together) come in at the same time. Also of value is to have small groups meet with me during office hours. For an hour I might meet with five or six students for an open discussion on any topics they choose to raise. This is a good way to get personal contact and to sense how students are perceiving the course. Their input in these informal small group sessions has led to modifications in the course, and these meetings have given students a chance to have some part in the development of the course. If a course is not moving as well as it could be, discussing this issue with students in these small groups can help to identify the sources of problems, which can then be corrected, at times with only minor modifications.

9. One of the group counseling courses at our university can be repeated for credit. The rationale for this is that students learn something different the second time they lead a group, and the content in the course is different for these advanced students. I've found that it helps to have second-semester students, especially if they are paired with new students. This opens the door for peer teaching, which can be extremely effective in this kind of class. I've found that extra time with the second-semester students can help them function as teaching-assistants in some sense. I am involved in a process of supervision with these advanced students, and they are learning how to be consultants for their peers.

10. There are two professional organizations that I find valuable for instructors of group counseling courses:

    a. The Association for Specialists in Group Work, a division of the American Association for Counseling and Development. All ASGW members receive the *Journal for Specialists in Group Work,* a quarterly journal that publishes research, practical, and innovative articles in the field of group work. Members also receive: (a) the *ASGW Together* which provides both regional and national information and special articles of interest to group practitioners; (b) the *Journal of Counseling and Development;* and (c*) Counseling Today,* a monthly newspaper. Students enrolled in counseling or human services programs and who have an interest in group work are able to join ASGW and ACA at reduced rates by contacting the ACA Membership Division, 5999 Stevenson Avenue, Alexandria, Virginia 22304, or telephone (800) 347-6647. Each spring the national convention of ACA meets and offers a variety of pre-convention workshops.

b. The American Group Psychotherapy Association (AGPA), an organization that sponsors a national convention each February. Before the convention, members can participate in two-day workshops in psychodynamic groups (and other group orientations) and attend full- and half-day workshops in group therapy during the convention. I've found the AGPA institutes and workshops to be very stimulating. This organization publishes a quarterly journal, *International Journal of Group Psychotherapy,* and a newsletter as well. The AGPA does have a student-member category. Information is available from the American Group Psychotherapy Association, Inc., 25 East 21st Street, 6th Floor, New York, New York 10010, or telephone (212) 477-2677.

11. It is important that you decide on your priorities. In preparing the material for this manual, I am aware that there is more material than can be covered in any single course, whether on the graduate or the undergraduate level. My attempt is to provide you with an abundance of material in this manual so that you can select whatever seems to be most workable for you. Likewise, in the *Student Manual,* there are many suggested activities, more than can be covered in one course. Students and instructors can decide on their priorities and then select those questions, exercises, and activities that tie into these priorities.

12. **A New Package.** As of 1999, a new video on group counseling, *Evolution of a Group,* is available for student purchase. An accompanying student workbook is an integral part of the video. The workbook guides students through the video so that they can get the maximum learning benefit from viewing the video and using the workbook as a companion. Together, the video and workbook are an interactive program to be used for self-study with a group counseling textbook, such as *Theory and Practice of Group Counseling, Fifth Edition.* The video and the workbook emphasize the application of concepts and techniques appropriate to the various stages of a group's development. The workbook requires that students become active learners as they study group process in action. The video and workbook are published by Brooks/Cole · Wadsworth Publishing Company.

Key features of the student workbook that accompanies the video are:

- A previewing self-inventory

- A group leadership skills checklist

- Process commentary elaborating on interventions made with individuals and facilitating the group process

- A summary of key themes for each stage of group that you will see in the video, member functions, and leaders functions

- A strategy for drawing on a variety of techniques
- Questions to consider in understanding group process
- Questions to consider for various segments of work
- Exercises and activities to complete
- A commentary on the issues surrounding the work done by individual members and group process developments
- A follow-up self-inventory at the end of the program
- A list of references for further reading

Evolution of a Group is a new concept in training of group workers. The video is designed to bring to life the unfolding of a group and illustrates a group as it evolves from the initial to final stage. This two-hour educational video shows a weekend residential group co-facilitated by Gerald Corey and Marianne Schneider Corey—and the *new Chapter 17* in *Theory and Practice of Group Counseling* is based on this actual group shown in the video. The group workshop included people who were real group members willing to explore their own issues and concerns. They were neither actors following a script, nor were they role-playing the topics.

Evolution of a Group depicts central features that will help students understand group dynamics at the various stages of a group: initial, transition, working, and final stages. Group leadership techniques are demonstrated as are interactions among the members at each of the stages of the group.

After viewing the video, and completing the student workbook that accompanies this video, students will be better able to:

a. Identify the major characteristics of each of the stages of a group.
b. Be able to apply certain techniques in opening and closing a group session.
c. Discuss the importance of focusing on the here-and-now interactions within a group.
d. Understand how past experiences can be worked with in the present.
e. Discuss the value of self-awareness in knowing your values and how they affect you as a group counselor.
f. Identify the major tasks of group leadership at each of the stages of a group.
g. Identify the major functions and roles of co-leaders.
h. Identify the roles and expectations of group members at the various stages of a group.

      i. Discuss how group leaders can effectively work with issues of cultural diversity in a group.

      j. Discuss building a climate of trust in a group setting.

      k. Discuss ways to formulate an agenda for a group session.

      l. Apply specific skills to help members formulate personal goals.

13. What is the purpose of the group counseling course? One of the group courses that I regularly teach is an undergraduate course, **Human Services 450, Theory and Practice of Group Counseling.** This course is a combination of didactic and experiential activities. Students are exposed to the ten theories of group work covered in *Theory and Practice of Group Counseling, Fifth Edition.* In the course outline, it is mentioned that the course consists of an intensive experience of both a theoretical and practical nature. The course entails supervised experience as a co-leader of groups, with opportunities for group supervision and discussion on the nature of the work of group leading. The goal of the course is to provide an integration of concepts and skills; theory is applied to actual practice of group work. To accomplish this, the course consists of: brief lectures on each theory (followed by a demonstration group and discussion of the demonstration), opportunities to co-lead groups with peers with supervision and ongoing feedback, participation in demonstrations of various group models, experiential practice in a weekly group, writing of reaction/thought/position papers, and doing extensive readings in group process.

14. **Course outline for Human Services 450, Theory and Practice of Group Counseling.** During the 16 weeks in a semester, we typically devote the first three weeks to introduction and overview of groups, ethics in group counseling, stages in the development of a group, and group leadership/group membership issues. *(See the course outline starting on the next page for details.)*

    During the rest of the semester, each of the sessions is structured around a particular theoretical approach to group work. The class meets twice a week for 75 minutes each meeting. On Tuesdays, students are in a small group and explore the personal applications of a specific theory each week. For the first 45 minutes, two students co-lead the group. During the last 30 minutes, the supervisor gives feedback and leads a discussion of what just took place. Each Tuesday a different student pair is responsible for facilitating the group. By the end of the semester, each student has had the opportunity to co-lead the group at least twice. On Thursdays prior to the small group, I give a lecture and conduct a demonstration group on the theory that will be explored the following Tuesday in their small groups. *(See the course outline for a detailed description of the schedule, focus topics, and suggested themes for each of the ten theories that might be productively explored in the Tuesday small groups.)*

HUSER 450
Theory and Practice of Group Counseling

Tuesday and Thursday: 10:00 to 11:15
Dr. Jerry Corey, *Professor of Human Services*
California State University, Fullerton

I. *Catalog Description:* Prerequisites: **Huser 300 and 380** and **Consent of Instructor.** A critical evaluation of ten contemporary theoretical approaches to group counseling and basic issues in group work. Emphasis is upon developing skills, under supervised conditions, and applying theories and techniques to actual group situations.

II. *Rationale for the Course.* The course is primarily intended as an elective for Human Services majors who desire increased knowledge and skill in the various models of group counseling. **Huser 450** will be a combination of didactic *and* experiential elements which will include lectures, discussions, demonstrations, videos, experiential opportunities in groups, and supervised practice in co-leading groups in the classroom situation. The class is designed to meet two times weekly. One of these days will be devoted to providing each student with opportunities to co-lead peer groups under direct supervision. One of the meetings each week will be set aside for lecture, discussion, and critique of key concepts and practical applications. The instructor will lead a demonstration group, which will be followed up by a discussion of the entire class.

III. *Required Textbooks for* **Huser 450** *

1. *Theory and Practice of Group Counseling* (5th Edition, 2000)

2. *Manual for Theory and Practice of Group Counseling*

3. Suggested only: Video—*Evolution of a Group* (Accompanied by Student Workbook)

* It is absolutely essential to read the assigned chapters (in both *Theory and Practice of Group Counseling* [*TPGC*] textbook and the *Student Manual*) by the due date. Generally, **each Thursday** the take-home quiz to a specific theory will be due. For the QUIZ you are expected to turn in the Pre-Chapter Self-Inventory and the Comprehension Check (Quiz) on a separate answer sheet. On **each Tuesday** a two-page reflection paper for each theory is due.

SCHEDULE OF TOPICS, READINGS, AND PAPERS
Week Number: (1) to (16)

1. **INTRODUCTION TO GROUP WORK** (Ch. 1)
   ETHICAL ISSUES (Read Chs. 1, 2 and 3)
   Thursday: Lecture/Discussion on **ASGW Guidelines for Group Counselors**. Complete exercises and inventories in Chs. 2 and 3 of **Student Manual** and be ready to discuss ethical issues.

2. **STAGES OF GROUP DEVELOPMENT**
   Early Stages of Group (Read Ch. 4 of *TPGC* text and manual)
   Video: *Evolution of a Group*

3. **STAGES OF GROUP DEVELOPMENT**
   Later Stages of Group (Read Ch. 5 of *TPGC* text and manual)
   Video: *Evolution of a Group*

4. **Begin Small Groups**
   Focus on Identifying Personal Goals for Your Groups
   Thursday: Lecture/Discussion on Psychoanalytic Groups
   Reading of Chapter 6 due
   Turn in QUIZ pp. 68–70 on Psychoanalytic Group and Pre-Chapter Self-Inventory

5. **PSYCHOANALYTIC GROUP** (Ch. 6)
   Tuesday: Small Groups on Psychoanalytic
   Reflection Paper #1 on Psychoanalytic Group due on Tuesday
   Thursday: Lecture/Discussion on Adlerian Group (Ch. 7)
   Turn in QUIZ pp. 79–81 on Adlerian Group and Pre-Chapter Self-Inventory

6. **ADLERIAN GROUP** (Ch. 7 of text and manual)
   Tuesday: Small Groups on Adlerian
   Reflection Paper #2 on Adlerian Group due on Tuesday
   Thursday: Lecture/Discussion on Psychodrama (Ch. 8)
   Turn in QUIZ pp. 89–91 on Psychodrama and Pre-Chapter Self-Inventory

7. **PSYCHODRAMA** (Ch. 8 of text and manual)
   Tuesday: Small Groups on Psychodrama
   Reflection Paper #3 on Psychodrama Group due on Tuesday
   Thursday: Lecture/Discussion on Existential (Ch. 9)
   Turn in QUIZ pp. 100–101 on Existential Group and Pre-Chapter Self-Inventory

8. **EXISTENTIAL** Group (Ch. 9 text and manual)
   Tuesday: Small Groups on Existential
   Reflection Paper #4 on Existential Group due on Tuesday
   Thursday: Lecture/Discussion on Gestalt Group (Ch. 11)
   Turn in QUIZ pp. 120–122 on Gestalt Group and Pre-Chapter Self-Inventory

9. **PERSON-CENTERED GROUP** (Ch. 10 of text/manual)
   Tuesday: Small Groups on Person-Centered Group (PCT)
   Reflection Paper #5 on PCT Group due on Tuesday
   Thursday: Lecture/Discussion on Transactional Analysis (TA) Groups (Ch. 12)
   Turn in QUIZ pp. 131–133 on TA Groups and Pre-Chapter Self-Inventory

10. **GESTALT GROUP** (Ch. 11 of text and manual)
    Tuesday: Small Groups on Gestalt
    Reflection Paper #6 on Gestalt Group due on Tuesday
    Thursday: Lecture/Discussion on PCT Groups (Ch. 10)
    Turn in QUIZ pp. 109–111 on Person Centered Group and Pre-Chapter Self-Inventory

11. **TRANSACTIONAL ANALYSIS GROUP** (Ch. 12 of text and manual)
    Tuesday: Small Groups on TA Group
    Reflection Paper #7 on TA Group due on Tuesday
    Thursday: Lecture/Discussion on Behavioral Groups (Ch. 13)
    Turn in QUIZ pp. 144–145 on Behavioral Groups and Pre-Chapter Self-Inventory

12. **BEHAVIORAL GROUP** (Ch. 13 of text and manual)
    Tuesday: Small Group on Behavioral
    Reflection Paper #8 on Behavioral Group due on Tuesday
    Thursday: Lecture/Discussion on REBT Groups (Ch. 14)
    Turn in QUIZ pp. 159–160 on REBT Groups and Pre-Chapter Self-Inventory

13. **RATIONAL EMOTIVE BEHAVIOR THERAPY GROUP (REBT)** (Ch. 14 text and manual)
    • **Paper for Huser 450 due**
    Tuesday: Small Group on REBT
    Reflection Paper #9 on REBT Group due on Tuesday
    Thursday: Lecture/Discussion on Reality Therapy (Ch. 15)
    Turn in QUIZ pp. 173–175 on Reality Groups and Pre-Chapter Self-Inventory.

14. **REALITY THERAPY GROUP** (RT) (Ch. 15 text and manual)
    Tuesday: Small Groups on RT
    Reflection Paper #10 on Reality Therapy Group due on Tuesday
    Thursday: **APPLICATION AND INTEGRATION OF APPROACHES** (Chs. 16 and 17) and Review of the Stages of Your Groups and Student Evaluations

15. **CONSOLIDATION OF LEARNINGS**
    Tuesday: Last Small Group Meeting
    Discussion of the Group Process
    • Meeting with the Entire Class: The Highlights of the Group Process and Consolidation of Personal Learnings

16. **FINAL EXAMINATION**
    The final is an objective test and consists of a comprehensive 200-item examination covering all of *TPGC* and it constitutes one-third of your final course grade.

FOCUS TOPICS FOR TUESDAY GROUPS
Purpose of the Tuesday Groups for Huser 450. The main purpose of the Tuesday 450 group is to give you a chance to learn about ways of applying the basic ideas and techniques to group work from the perspective of a member and a leader. The experiential practice is primarily for learning about group process, and thus, it is not a therapy group. **Do keep a good record of your reactions to this experience and process notes about the group in your journal,** as you will be expected to write about your experience in this group, as well as your learnings from observing these groups in class.

Expectations We will discuss the theory on Thursday (prior to the day you practice with a given theory in your groups on Tuesday). Each of you are expected to have **read the assigned chapter** and worked through the material in the corresponding chapter in the *Student Manual* on the assigned dates in the course outline, which is usually a Thursday, before the small groups meet on that theory. The Thursday session will be devoted largely to lecture, discussion, and demonstration of the theory that week—after you have had an opportunity to experience and practice the theory in a small group. The Tuesday session will generally consist of small groups focusing on the theory under study, with opportunities for students to co-lead a small group with supervision and feedback. After the group session, time will be allocated for processing and discussing the group.

As members, each of you are expected to decide upon a small and realistic goal that will guide your active participation. Think of a personal issue relative to each model that has relevance to your effectiveness as a group facilitator. Consider what you know about yourself that is likely to directly influence your ability to facilitate the work of others. What might get in your way? Again, *the purpose of this group is not to provide therapy,* thus the personal concern you bring to each session should be manageable within the limits of the group session. As co-leaders, do your best to stay within the general spirit of the group model you have selected, but take the cues for the direction you will pursue from the members. To give a clearer sense of the focus of these small groups, a suggested theme is listed below for each of the weeks.

SCHEDULE OF TUESDAY GROUPS
Topics for Getting You Focused for Participation
NOTE: The theories are to be read and studied, and both the *TPGC* text and *Student Manual* are to be completed for the given theory on **Tuesday** of each week. **Thursdays** are generally devoted to didactic work on applying the theory to practice, and class discussion of the theory. **Tuesdays** typically

include opportunities for students to co-lead within the framework of a particular modality. **Reflection papers** are due each Tuesday on each of the ten theories. We will rely on the exercises in the *Student Manual* for material for exploration in the group sessions.

Topics for the Tuesday Groups

Weeks 1–3: During the **first three weeks** of class we will meet as an entire class. Small groups begin on the fourth week.

Week 4—**Establishing Personal Goals**
Identify specific goals that will guide your participation in the small groups for the semester. (For this first small group meeting, the supervisors will facilitate the sessions).

Week 5—**Psychoanalytic Group**
Focus on areas of potential **countertransferences** that are likely to affect your work as a co-leader. What are some of the main ways you are likely to display **resistance,** and how might you challenge your resistance? What is an example of one of your major **defenses** when you experience anxiety?

Week 6—**Adlerian Group**
Focus on some of the main ways that your **family of origin has influenced you**—the person that you are today. What are some ways that your early experiences in **your family might be replayed in the groups** in which you participate now as a member or as a leader?

Week 7—**Psychodrama**
Focus on some interpersonal relationship that you would like to improve. Role-playing techniques can be applied to working on relationship concerns.

Week 8—**Existential Group**
Focus on how you are dealing with **freedom and responsibility** in your own life at this time. How is your ability to cope with freedom and responsibility in a personal way a factor in your ability to facilitate your groups? Focus on how you are in the here-and-now in this group.

Week 9—**Person-Centered Group**
Focus on the nature of your experience at this time in your groups. What might you like to change in yourself? What are your main reactions to the experience of this group, and what ways might you want to be different? Focus on identifying what you want for yourself in your groups.

Week 10—**Gestalt Group**
Focus on any **unfinished business from your personal life** that might be getting in the way of your effectiveness in co-leading your group. Identify one area of unfinished business that you would like to complete. You might also explore a central polarity in your life and reflect on ways you would want to integrate what appears to be diverse dimensions of yourself.

Week 11—**Transactional Analysis Group**
Focus on the **injunctions** that you heard (verbally and nonverbally), and especially think about one of your early decisions. After identifying **a central early decision,** ask the degree to which this decision still serves you. How does this decision affect you as a group leader? What **new decision** might you consider?

Week 12—**Behavioral Group**
Focus on a **specific behavior pattern** that you would like to change—some thoughts/beliefs, or ways of acting, or some feeling. What is the impact of this behavior pattern on your work as a group leader? How might you go about making the change you say you want to make?

Week 13—**Rational Emotive Behavior Therapy Group**
Reflect on **your internal dialogue as a group leader and/or as a group member** and identify **one major belief** that you see as being dysfunctional. What self-talk or cognitions most get in your way? What are some ways that you can **practice challenging an irrational belief** and substituting more constructive ways of thinking?

Week 14—**Reality Therapy Group**
Focus on some of the main things that you learned about yourself in all of your groups this semester. What is **one form of behavior** that you would very much like **to change**? Take a look at any unfinished business.

Week 15—**Last Small Group Session**
The focus of this session is a review of the evolution of your group and what you learned about group process from the experience of your Tuesday group. Emphasis of this session is on discussion of turning points in your group and consolidation of your learnings as a group member. See below for guidelines for processing your learnings:

What did you learn about yourself from participating in this group? What specific attitudes and behaviors could either help or hinder you as a group leader?

- Review your personal goals that you identified at the first session and assess the degree to which you have met these goals in the Tuesday group. Where might you want to go from here?

- What are some potential countertransference issues that may have surfaced? Any unresolved personal concerns that you still need to explore? Any plans regarding where you can go from here?

- What are some specific skills that you acquired that will be useful to you as a group leader? How about as a group member?

What did you learn about group process from participating in this group?

- How would you describe the "personality of your group?" How did you tend to interact with one another?

- What did the experience of the small groups teach you about how groups function and malfunction? What have you learned from this experience that you can apply to some future group you may lead?

- What stages did your group go through? Focus on issues such as the development of trust, formulating goals and agendas, dealing with supervision, shifting of roles between leader and member, recognizing and dealing with conflict, and dealing with potential forms of resistance. What turning points characterized your group?

COURSE REQUIREMENTS AND GRADING PRACTICES
Requirements of Students
In order to be eligible for enrollment in Huser 450, students must have successfully completed Huser 300 and Huser 380. Consent of instructor is also required. The present course is an advanced course that aims at integrating theory and practice, as well as teaching students a basic framework they can use in applying selected concepts and techniques from the contemporary theories to groups. Other specific requirements are listed below:

- Active participation in class discussions and workshops

- Prompt attendance at *all* the class sessions

- Keeping up-to-date with all of the assigned readings

- Keeping a journal with a focus on your reactions to group

- Final integrative paper

- Take-home reflection papers turned in for each theory on time (10 reflection papers worth 100 points maximum)

- Take-home Quizzes and Pre-Chapter Self-Inventory for each of the 10 theories (100 points)

- Final Examination (200 points)

Basis for Grading
Your grade for this course will be determined by evidence of the quality of your learning as demonstrated by your performance in the following areas:

- One-third of grade is based on the final integrative paper

- One-third of grade is based on the combination of 10 Take-home Quizzes (100 points) *and* 10 reflection papers (100 points) for a maximum of 200 points and is converted into a percentage grade.

- One-third of grade is based on the Final Examination (200 points) which is converted into a percentage grade.

Quizzes for Theories
You get *10 points for each* of the Quizzes and the Pre-Chapter Self-Inventories if they are submitted on time (Thursday), and if you have attended the class meeting for each of the 10 theories.

Weekly Reflection Papers
There are 10 weekly reflection papers due, each of which should be two double-spaced typewritten pages. Each of these papers are worth 10 points maximum. 10 = Outstanding or excellent; 9=Very good; 8=Satisfactory, but could use improvement. To earn credit for a reflection paper it is expected that it will be *turned in* at the *beginning* of the Tuesday small group session when it is due.

Attendance/Class Participation
You are expected to be an active learner, which includes verbally participating in both the class and group discussions. You are also expected to bring questions for discussion to the class sessions and demonstrate that you are keeping up to date with your reading assignments.

NOTE: Although part of your course grade may be influenced by your participation in the class discussions, there will be no points assigned for this component. It should be noted that you are not graded or evaluated on the basis of your participation in the small groups—either in the member or leader roles. In other words, the quantity and quality of your self-exploration and progress in self-awareness and personal growth are *not* factors weighed in your course grade. Please review the guidelines for getting the most from participating in a group, *"Ways of Getting the Most From A Group Experience,"* which is given in the *Student Manual* (Chapter 1).

ATTENDANCE at full duration of class is expected at each class meeting, unless you have an emergency situation or are really ill. For me to credit you with an EXCUSED ABSENCE, you need to know that it is YOUR RESPONSIBILITY to inform me of such cases immediately upon returning to class. Absences and tardiness will be a factor in determining your participation/attendance grade; excessive absences or tardiness might result in getting a full grade deducted (or in some cases even failing the course). **To be able to get credit for the weekly quizzes, you must attend the class session.** I do expect you to function as a professional in any agency, which means showing up and participating!

PARTICIPATION is a MUST in this course. If you are not willing to get actively involved in sharing/exchanging your ideas on issues, then you should consider *not taking* this class. This class will involve some degree of self-exploration and interpersonal learning. Again, if you have serious reservations about becoming personally involved in a group process, or if you do not want to be challenged emotionally, then do not enroll in this class. The assumption is that one of the best ways to learn about the practice of group counseling is to experience the process and then conceptualize this learning experience. We will talk more fully about the guidelines for self-disclosure and the expectations at the first class meeting.

Group Leader's Journal
A basic requirement of Huser 450 is that you keep an ongoing and up-to-date journal with a focus on your personal experiences and learnings related to the various facets of the course. This journal will be useful in integrating your learnings and will be especially helpful in writing your papers. The journal will be a way for you to keep track of your personal journey in this course as well as highlight conceptual learnings.

Grading Scale: (percentage)
100–98 = A+
97–94 = A
93–91 = A-
90–88 = B+
87–84 = B
83–81 = B-
80–78 = C+
77–74 = C
73–71 = C-
70–68 = D+
67–64 = D
63–61 = D-
Below 60 = F

GUIDELINES FOR FINAL INTEGRATIVE HUSER 450 PAPER

The final integrative paper makes up *one-third* of your course grade. LATE PAPERS generally have a penalty of at least -15% deduction from the total (if only a few days late). For example, if you were to receive a 93% on a paper, yet submit it late, if would be docked 15%, which would yield a 79% for the paper. The paper should be TYPED and double-spaced, CAREFULLY PROOFREAD, and should give evidence of considerable thought/outside reading, and must show development of your positions in a coherent, logical, creative, and organized way. There are two parts to your paper, for a total length of about 20 pages.

Part 1
Do an integrative paper based on some of the ten theories of group counseling. These theories include: **psychoanalytic, Adlerian, psychodrama, existential, Gestalt, Person-centered therapy, Transactional Analysis, behavior therapy, rational emotive behavior therapy,** and **reality therapy.** Write an integrative paper that articulates your **personal theoretical orientation to group counseling.** Your paper should deal with aspects such as: (1) key concepts of your approach, (2) view of your role as a group counselor, (3) role of group members, (4) key developmental tasks and

therapeutic goals, (5) techniques and methods, and (6) stages in the evolution of a group. Address specific issues as outlined in the *TPGC* textbook and *Student Manual,* especially Chapter 17. Chapter 17 contains some summary charts that will be useful. In the *Student Manual,* there is a two-page summary chart of the initial, working, and final stage of a group as applied to each theory.

This particular essay should be **about 12 pages** (double-spaced, with standard font and margins). You should attempt to integrate as many concepts and techniques as you can based upon several of the models of group counseling. DO NOT give a summary of textbook content. Demonstrate that you understand the various models by looking for common denominators among several therapy approaches. For example, you might cluster some theories together and address common concepts and themes associated with a general category of theories:

1. Psychodynamic approaches (psychoanalytic and Adlerian)
2. Experiential and relationship-oriented approaches (existential, person-centered, existential, and Gestalt)
3. Cognitive-behavioral approaches (TA, behavior therapy, REBT, and reality therapy)

If you do this, you are really integrating no more than three general approaches. Show how you might use key concepts and techniques from the various approaches in working with diverse client populations in a group setting. It is important that you address the implications of your personalized approach to effective multicultural practice, so do incorporate the diversity perspective in your presentation.

You do not need to cover *all* of the theories, for this is too ambitious in 12 pages. What you want to accomplish is to demonstrate YOUR OWN INTEGRATION of several different approaches—or you could even take a single main theory as your basic theory as an anchor, and then demonstrate how you would draw techniques from the other approaches. You might also want to apply your integrative theory to a particular client population or a particular type of group. See Chapter 17 of *TPGC* text for ideas, but *do not copy* my personal integrative approach as your approach. Be original and show that you are able to synthesize, integrate, and conceptualize a model that will help you work more effectively as a group leader. Also, see the two-page charts (Stages in the Development) that are given in each of the different theory chapters in the *Student Manual* (about 12 pages).

Part 2

Process your own group experience. Write **about an eight-page essay** on both your personal learnings and on the group process aspects based on your participation in your Tuesday group for this semester. What did you learn about yourself (specifically) through this process? Focus on the qualities about yourself that might either enhance or detract from your effectiveness as a group leader. Concretely, what did this group experience teach you about being a group member? about group leadership? about how groups function or malfunction? about the stages of a group? about techniques? about ways to deal effectively with conflict? about the value of support and confrontation? about ways of building a trusting community?

Address what you learned from the process of dealing with different theoretical approaches to group work. Describe in clear terms your main learnings based on the exploration of various approaches in your labs. Discuss the characteristics that applied to your group and show how your group did or did not fit the characteristics described in the readings, especially in Chapters 4 and 5. (This part should be about 8 pages.)

INFORMATION ON COREY BOOKS AND VIDEOS

Below is a listing of books and videos by Gerald Corey and Marianne Schneider Corey from Brooks/Cole • Wadsworth:

Theory and Practice of Group Counseling, 5th Edition (2000, Gerald Corey)

Student Manual for Theory and Practice of Group Counseling, 5th Edition (2000, Gerald Corey)

* *Student Video—Evolution of a Group* (2000, Gerald Corey, Marianne Schneider Corey, and Robert Haynes) (two hours)

* *Student Workbook for Evolution of a Group* (2000, Gerald Corey, Marianne Schneider Corey, and Robert Haynes)

> * Student video and workbook for *Evolution of a Group* packaged together for sale to students ISBN: 0-534-36324-5 (Net Price: $26.00)

+ *Facilitator's Resource Manual for Ethics in Action* (1998, Gerald Corey, Marianne Schneider Corey, and Robert Haynes)

+ *Institutional Video—Ethics in Action* (1998, Gerald Corey, Marianne Schneider Corey, and Robert Haynes) (one hour)

> + Institutional version video of *Ethics in Action* is accompanied by Facilitator's Resource Manual ISBN: 0-534-35621-4 (Net Price: $130.00)

++ *Student Video—Ethics in Action* (1998, Gerald Corey, Marianne Schneider Corey, and Robert Haynes) (1 hour)

++ *Student Workbook for Ethics in Action* (1998, Gerald Corey, Marianne Schneider Corey, and Robert Haynes)

> ++ Student video and workbook for *Ethics in Action* packaged together for sale to students ISBN: 0-534-35619-2 (Net Price: $21.00)

Issues and Ethics in the Helping Professions, 5th Edition (1998, Gerald Corey, Marianne Schneider Corey, and Patrick Callanan) ISBN: 0-534-34689-8 (Accompanied by Instructor's Resource Manual and Transparency Masters)

Becoming a Helper, 3rd Edition (1998, Marianne Schneider Corey and Gerald Corey) ISBN: 0-534-35460-2 (Accompanied by Instructor's Resource Manual and Transparency Masters)

Living and Learning (Gerald Corey, Cindy Corey, and Heidi Jo Corey, 1997). Accompanied by an Instructor's Resource Manual and an 8-minute video entitled Living and Learning ISBN: 0-534-50500-7

I Never Knew I Had a Choice, 6th Edition (1997, Gerald Corey and Marianne Schneider Corey)   ISBN: 0-534-34340-6   (Accompanied by Instructor's Resource Manual)

Groups: Process and Practice, 5th Edition (1997, Marianne Schneider Corey and Gerald Corey) ISBN: 0-534-34224-8 (Accompanied by Instructor's Resource Manual)

Case Approach to Counseling and Psychotherapy, 4th Edition (1996, Gerald Corey) ISBN: 0-534-26580-4

Theory and Practice of Counseling and Psychotherapy, 5th Edition (1996, Gerald Corey)   ISBN: 0-534-33856-9   (Accompanied by Instructor's Resource Manual and Transparency Masters)

Student Manual for Theory and Practice of Counseling and Psychotherapy, 5th Edition (1996, Gerald Corey) ISBN: 0-534-33858-7

The Art of Integrative Counseling and Psychotherapy: Videos 1 and 2
** Video 1: Techniques in Action (one hour)
   ISBN: 0-534-33898-4 (Net price: $183.95)
** Video 2: Challenges for the Counselor (27 minutes)
   ISBN: 0-534-34098-9 (Net Price: $94.95)

> ** Video set: Both videos 1 and 2. ISBN: 0-534-34099-7 (Net Price: $262.95)   (Accompanied by Facilitator's Guide [ISBN: 0-534-34100-4])

Group Techniques, 2nd Edition (1992, Gerald Corey, Marianne Schneider Corey, Patrick Callanan, and J. Michael Russell) ISBN: 0-534-16248-7

A Demo Video Package featuring clips from all of the above Corey videos is available to instructors who are considering adoption of any of these videos. For more information, please contact your Brooks/Cole-Wadsworth representative at (800) 423-0563. ISBN: 0-534-37047-0 (30 minutes)

For a copy of the lastest Brooks/Cole · Wadsworth Human Services, Counseling, and Social Work Catalog contact:

Brooks/Cole Publishing Company
Source Code 8BCCNM01
511 Forest Lodge Road
Pacific Grove, CA 93950-5098
Phone: (800) 423-0563
Fax: (408) 375-6414
e-mail: info@brookscole.com
Internet: http://www.brookscole.com

Gerald Corey is also co-author, with Barbara Herlihy, of two books published by the American Counseling Association:

Boundary Issues in Counseling: Multiple Roles and Responsibilities (1997) Order # 72637 (ACA member price: $17.95)

ACA Ethical Standards Casebook, 5th Edition (1996) Order #72621 (ACA member price: $19.95)

To order either *Boundary Issues in Counseling* or *ACA Ethical Standards Casebook,* call ACA at (800) 422-2648.

PART II
Perspectives and Practices on the Education and Training of Group Leaders

PART II
Perspectives and Practices on the Education and Training of Group Leader

The issues of what constitutes the essential components of a program for the education and training of competent group leaders is of central interest to professionals in the field of group counseling. In this section I describe my views on this issue and summarize the views of other writers who have developed guidelines and standards for training programs. For this purpose I shall draw on a course I regularly teach—*Practicum in Group Leadership*—at California State University at Fullerton.

Prerequisites
Human Services 490 (*Practicum in Group Leadership*) requires that students co-lead a personal-development, self-exploratory course at the university. Therefore, I screen candidates before the course begins, to determine whether their personal characteristics are suitable for this kind of work and whether they are ready to undertake the demanding tasks that group leading involves. The screening interview gives the candidate an opportunity to find out about the nature and requirements of the course, to meet with and ask questions to students already enrolled in the group, and to ask me any questions he or she has regarding the course.

Foundations and Course-work Background
Another prerequisite for admission into the *Practicum in Group Leadership* is the successful completion of a group-oriented personal-growth course that explores such personal issues as autonomy, life choices, meaning and values, work, love/sex/intimacy, sex roles, loneliness, death, and other areas of interest to the student. It is this course that the prospective group leader will eventually co-lead and that will constitute his or her supervised field experience in group work. Also, students must take a course in theories and techniques of counseling (an overview of the major models of individual counseling). Ideally, students are also required to complete Human Services 450 (*Theory and Practice of Group Counseling*) prior to enrolling in Human Services 490 (*Practicum in Group Leadership*). They may also enroll in both of these courses concurrently.

Didactic Course Work
The course that I teach for group leaders consists in part of brief lecture presentations, a great deal of class discussion and interaction, student presentations, and participation in demonstration groups. The content deals with the stages of a group's development and group process concepts. Generally, we devote about two to three weeks on each of these stages: formation of groups; initial stage; transition stage; working stage; final stage; and groups for special populations. For this course, the required textbooks are: (1) Corey and Corey (1997) *Groups: Process and Practice;* and (2) Corey, Corey, Callanan, and Russell (1992) *Group Techniques*. This course

addresses core issues from the forming of groups to the termination of groups.

Supervised Practice
In my judgment, the heart of a training program for group leaders is practice in leading groups under adequate supervision and with a co-leader. Feedback from the supervisor and from the co-leader can help trainees recognize mistakes and detect areas they are overlooking. Feedback should also call attention to the trainees' strengths so that the student leaders can build on them.

A feedback technique that I use, and one that reduces defensiveness on the part of the trainees, is to focus on the alternative procedures that could have been employed. This is a useful feedback technique, since it is generally not a question of taking the "right" or "wrong" approach but, rather, a question of determining which approach is the best one for a specific aim or circumstance. Thus, I tend to challenge trainees to reflect on what they did or didn't do, how they made certain interventions and why, what alternative procedures and approaches they might have used, and what they might be missing concerning the group dynamics. My trainees seem to find this approach constructive; it takes the focus off the detection-of-mistakes approach —an approach that may lead to the trainees' becoming excessively self-conscious, which, in turn, can interfere with their ability to freely apply what they know as they are leading their groups.

Trainees in the *Practicum in Group Leadership* are required to act as co-leaders for a semester in a small group under the supervision of a professor (typically a licensed counselor or some other professional in the field of Human Services) who teaches an introductory personal-growth, group-oriented course that is required for all the Human Services majors. This supervising professor meets with the leader trainees before and after the class to plan sessions and to provide group supervision; he or she also spends time observing the students while they are co-leading their groups.

WEEKEND WORKSHOPS AND ALL-DAY WORKSHOPS FOR TRAINING AND SUPERVISION

As a basic part of the *Practicum in Group Leadership* course, the students attend a three-day training and supervision workshop in group process. This is a somewhat structured workshop that gives students several opportunities to co-lead a small group of their peers and many opportunities for constructive feedback on their dual roles in the workshop as leaders and as members. The weekend of small-group work under direct supervision allows students to explore personal issues that can impact their effectiveness as group leaders. At the same time, it provides students with a means to learn how groups function by actually experiencing a group.

The following description is an adaptation of the article "Experiential/ Didactic Training and Supervision Workshop for Group Leaders," by

Marianne Schneider Corey and Gerald Corey, which appeared in the *Journal of Counseling and Human Service Professions,* May 1986.

Description of the Workshop

Several of my colleagues join me as supervisors at a weekend experiential/didactic workshop. This three-day workshop is something that my colleagues and I provide each semester without financial compensation. Although setting up and doing this kind of training workshop does take time and effort, the results make this investment worth it. The students pay only for the meals for the weekend, and they obtain one semester unit of credit for the 30-hour residential experience. The weekend workshop is scheduled early in the semester so that students can use what they learn in the workshop in their group class and in their leading of a group. I have already arranged to meet with all the prospective students (as a class) toward the end of the semester before they enroll in the group leadership course. At the first class meeting I describe the purpose and structure of the upcoming workshop. This advance planning allows for screening, selection, and orientation of the students who will participate in this special type of class. It also allows students to do the course reading before the new semester actually begins. This orientation process gives students a good idea of what is expected of them, and should they not want to commit themselves to this type of learning, they have plenty of opportunity to decide not to enroll in the course. We think that students should be aware of what the workshop entails before they commit themselves to this training experience, particularly of the expectation that they will become involved in a personal way by exploring personal concerns in their training group. The nature of this experience includes the following:

Participants will be involved as *both* group members and leaders in a small group during the weekend. The training supervisors will rotate among the groups during the weekend and will provide feedback after each of the sessions. Participants will have several opportunities to co-lead their small group with the benefit of supervision. Instruction on group process will be an integral and ongoing part of the entire workshop. Participants are expected to become actively involved in the group experience, both as members and as co-leaders of a group. The idea behind the workshop is that people learn best and acquire the group leadership skills identified by the ASGW (1991) by participating in a working group with an experiential/didactic focus, in which they function both as members and as leaders with careful supervision.

Preparation and Orientation for the Workshop

We encourage participants to do some reading about group process and group leadership prior to the workshop. Readings that we often recommend include:

Yalom (1995), *Theory and Practice of Group Psychotherapy;* Yalom (1983), *Inpatient Group Psycotherapy;* Corey and Corey (1997*), Groups: Process and Practice, Fifth Edition;* Corey, Corey, Callanan, and Russell (1992), *Group Techniques;* and Corey (2000), *Theory and Practice of Group Counseling, Fifth Edition.*

Our perspective on training stresses the importance of group leaders using themselves as therapeutic instruments. For us, the group leader's personal characteristics and behavior in group are far more important than any technique he or she may employ. By doing some reading prior to the workshop, participants acquire a cognitive framework to make sense of what they experience in their small group and thus are better able to apply the principles of leadership and membership in their group.

Participants have several opportunities to co-lead a small group with another participant. After co-leading their group, they receive feedback from other members and from us (the supervisors). During the times allocated for discussion of group process and feedback, the emphasis is upon constructive suggestions and openness to learning about themselves and how groups function. We provide some structure that facilitates learning about how groups function. We find that the best teaching occurs after participants have been involved in their small-group session and when the discussion grows out of actual events in the group. The workshop is *experiential,* in that the participants are expected to share and explore personal and interpersonal issues in the presence of peers and with our direct supervision. The workshop is also *didactic,* in that much of the time is devoted to conceptualizing what occurs in the context of their small group and to discussing group dynamics and ways of facilitating the group interactions. To make this learning more meaningful, the participants will be doing most of the leading at designated times.

Structure of the Training Workshop

The typical group class I offer is limited to about 24 students. For a group this size, there are six of us as training supervisors. We begin the workshop with some type of go-around for the purpose of learning names and sharing expectations for the weekend. We often ask people to pair up for about ten minutes to discuss such matters as their expectations, their hopes and fears, and what it was like for them to actually get to the workshop today. Members work in various dyads for about an hour or so. These short dyadic interactions facilitate their talking and listening and help them get to know one another in a relatively nonthreatening manner. After the dyads, we convene as an entire group to explore the participants' expectations and concerns. This is another way for people to get acquainted and is our means of establishing a climate conducive to open interaction.

The *Practicum in Group Leadership* class is typically composed of three groups. Each of these groups will work with another supervisor for fieldwork in group leading during the semester. The field supervisors who will work with the students all semester also volunteer their time to be a part of the weekend workshop. This arrangement allows the students to get to know one another and to develop a working relationship with their supervisor. In addition to their meeting with a field supervisor weekly and getting supervised group leading experience during the semester, the students meet with me each week for three hours in a group process class. Before the students come to the workshop,, they know they will remain together in their small groups for most of the workshop in order to experience the evolution of their group and to build cohesion within it. We also tell the students that we will rotate as supervisors in pairs. This allows them to work with six different supervisors, each of whom has a different background and leadership style.

Preparing Participants to Co-Lead Their Small Groups

While we are still together in the entire group, the six of us talk about our styles of supervision and offer some suggestions aimed at helping the participants get the maximum benefit from their experience, both as a member and as a facilitator of their small group. We urge them not to be overly concerned about making mistakes. We strongly recommend that they be active and involved and not to be passive and keep reactions to themselves. What they are thinking, feeling, perceiving, and experiencing in the here-and-now of a session is the very material that is best shared. We emphasize that there is no such thing as a "bad group," since everything that occurs in this kind of workshop is a resource for learning. We also allow some time for participants to express and explore their concerns, as well as ask us questions about the workshop. They often mention fear of getting stuck and not knowing what to do, concern about being left dangling, the difficulty they expect to face in switching from member to leader, wondering how far to go with personal issues, and their anxieties about the responsibility of co-leading a group. During this time we do our best to create a safe climate where the participants will feel free enough to practice leading and where they will feel trusting enough to share themselves in personal ways so that they can become a working group.

The Small-Group Sessions

During the first small-group session our main goal is to assist the participants to continue talking about any fears or expectations they have pertaining to the workshop. We encourage them to identify themselves to one another, which is partly done by defining their personal goals. Through getting acquainted in their small group, participants begin to actively create a trusting environment where they can engage in the self-disclosure necessary for a working group.

Another agenda we have for this session is to help the group come up with themes they can use as a focus for their sessions. Before the students come to the workshop, they know that each of the two-hour sessions will be structured around life themes taken from the book, *I Never Knew I Had a Choice* (Corey and Corey, Sixth Edition, 1997), which they have read in the earlier self-exploration group classes they took as a prerequisite to this course.

The workshop is structured around some of the following themes: reviewing your childhood and adolescence; the struggle toward autonomy; work and leisure; your body and stress management; sex roles; sexuality; intimate relationships; loneliness and solitude; death and loss, and meaning in life. The participants are not expected to stick rigidly to these themes in a given session; rather, these themes are points of departure and topics for focus. Generally, it is hoped that the student leaders learn that their own personal fears, problems, and unresolved issues will affect the way they lead groups. Other here-and-now issues surface and are then dealt with, especially such matters as the students' anxiety about not knowing enough to lead groups effectively; fears of being seen as incompetent; discomfort with intense emotions; fears of making mistakes; and concerns about being able to work well with a co-leader. We tend to focus on exploring self-defeating cognitions that these students bring to the workshop. For instance, many burden themselves with perfectionistic demands that they should already know everything there is to know about a group before they even take the class. They worry a great deal about their performance and how the supervisors will judge them. Some students are convinced that the supervisors will "discover them" and tell them they cannot continue in the course. They fear being exposed as incompetent. All these concerns make excellent material to work on in the sessions, for it is what is presently on many of their minds. Some of the most useful themes pertain to their concerns about doing well in this workshop and in the group course. We caution participants to avoid discussing such themes in abstract and impersonal ways, and we encourage the leaders to facilitate in a manner that will help members apply these themes to themselves and explore them in personal ways.

In a typical day there are about four small-group sessions, each lasting approximately two hours. The first hour is for group interaction time led by the participants co-leading in pairs. The second hour, which is led by the supervisors, is the time for critique, feedback, process commentary, and teaching. The group members become involved in this processing by talking about how they were affected during the session.

We encourage the student co-leaders to meet with each other before the session to discuss what has been going on in the group and to make plans for the session they will be co-leading. They are expected to open the group by looking for ways to involve as many participants as possible in the session. They facilitate the group and eventually bring the session to closure before our process commentary. We pay particular attention to how they open and close each session. They are largely responsible for the group for the hour, and we typically allow them to learn by struggling and trying new approaches.

At times we suggest a "time out" to briefly talk about some event in a group, particularly if it appears that the group is "stuck." We also encourage the co-leaders to stop the action by calling "time out" at any time that they want to confer aloud. We sometimes ask them to express what they are experiencing at the moment. This type of disclosure and discussion between co-leaders, done in the presence of the group, is often the very catalyst that starts a group moving again in a positive direction. Time and again they discover that what they reveal during this "time out" is the very thing they need to say in group.

During this first hour of group working time, we are taking notes that we later share with them. These details can serve as excellent teaching points during the process commentary time that immediately follows. Many aspects of what is going on in the group get our attention: How do the co-leaders open the group? How do they introduce techniques? If there is a theme, do the co-leaders facilitate group interaction and assist members to deal with the theme in a personal way? Are they also able to drop an agenda to pick up on an emerging theme in the group, such as lack of trust? What leadership skills are they demonstrating? Are they able to orchestrate member interaction, or do they focus on the person who speaks and ignore others? What are the results of certain interventions? Are they paying attention to nonverbal language? Are they able to move from one person to another in a natural way? What are the co-leaders modeling? How is conflict dealt with in the group? As to how the co-leaders are working together, are they competitive? Do they pick up on each other's interventions? What leadership skills do they need to acquire or refine? These are a few examples of what we focus on during the first hour. We find that the participants are most receptive to learning about group process when they have just experienced what we hope to teach.

The Process Commentary Time
The second hour of each small-group session begins with our request that the co-leaders talk to each other about what they were thinking and feeling during the past hour. As they express aloud their internal dialogue, the members are primed to react. We then ask the members to briefly summarize their experience. Then, as supervisor/trainers, we share our observations in such a way that they are encouraged to interact with us through questions and discussion. During the process commentary, we emphasize that there are many appropriate clues that can be picked up on and explored. What a leader decides to focus on is not a matter of "right" or "wrong"; rather, it is often a function of the leader's interest at the moment. Leaders might make a certain intervention (or avoid doing so) because of their theory, the lack of comfort with certain emotions, their personal blocks, or the mood that seems present in the group. We tend to focus on what the co-leaders had in mind with certain interventions and sometimes talk about alternative ways of intervening.

There are a number of common difficulties that we continue to observe in these small groups co-led by the participants. Because of their anxiety, co-leaders often make too many interventions in too short a time and don't give members enough time to respond to the interventions. Some have trouble connecting the work of one person with others in the room and they focus on an individual to the exclusion of the group. Some may drop a person rather abruptly and shift to someone else without a smooth transition. Many times the group assumes a problem-solving focus so that certain members may be pushed to find a solution to a problem before they have fully explored their feelings and thoughts about it. If these events occur in a session, they make great material for discussion.

During this process commentary time, we might ask co-leaders open-ended questions designed to help them reflect on their own experience as they were leading. Some of these key questions include: "What was going on with you when . . . ? Was there anything that you were aware of thinking or feeling but did not say? What hunches did you have when . . . ? Where might you go if you were to continue in the next session? Why did you introduce this particular technique at this time?" As we discuss the proceedings and provide feedback, we try to be constructive, honest, and sensitive. We encourage them to use whatever strengths they might have to build on and try not to discourage them from trying out new ideas and approaches. For example, if a leader is so active that she is actually interfering with the process, we would not tell her, "Wow, you sure blew it this time!" We might say, "I noticed that you were working very hard, and you really seemed to want something to happen. What was your perception?" We would reinforce her good intentions, and at the same time help her look at how her interventions got in the way and what she might be able to do differently in the future. At times we have to give difficult feedback, yet we say what needs to be said in a respectful and sensitive way. We notice that after the first small group and our process commentary, the participants relax greatly and feel much less anxiety. They watch the way we give feedback and see that we treat them with dignity. We respect their level of experience, whatever that may be, and give them room to learn by trial and error. Also, we encourage them to be patient with themselves and not burden themselves with unrealistic expectations of having to be perfect.

The Meetings with the Entire Group
Each day we spend some time meeting as a large group, primarily for sharing and discussing trends in each of the smaller groups. Members in each group give some kind of brief report of what is going on in their group. After these reports and the discussions that flow from them, we often do some further teaching about specific group process issues.

Leading by the Supervisors
We typically co-lead the small groups during the evening session. During these sessions, the participants have no leadership responsibilities. This is their time to bring up any issues that surfaced for them during the day, and to go further with them if they choose. Our leading provides a safeguard against members opening up issues without having a means to explore them in greater depth. The participants have an opportunity to work with any personal matters that are unsettled or with anyone in the workshop whom they might have reactions to. We realize that going from one session to another, being alternately a member of a group and a leader, working on a feeling level and then a cognitive level, and being in a personal working group and then shifting to a process-oriented discussion group can be unsettling and often demands adjustment. Our leading during the evening is one way of attending to the feelings that arise from the intense and demanding activities of a typical day in the workshop. It also gives the participants a chance to observe and experience each supervisor's style of leadership. However, we caution them against merely observing what we are doing and studying us. They are reminded that the best way to learn how to lead a group is by getting fully involved as a member, and then later conceptualizing and discussing what

they experienced. In the last small-group session, we also lead their groups and help them to review and integrate what they learned during the workshop. During this last review session, our focus can be discerned in the kinds of questions we suggest: "What did each of you learn about yourself as a member? As a leader? What stopped you? What facilitated you individually and as a group? What was helpful? Not helpful? How would it be if you had a group composed largely of members like yourself? What did you learn about group process that you can apply to groups you lead?" We are basically concerned with helping the participants review and consolidate their learnings, both about themselves personally and about how groups function.

We conclude the workshop by meeting as an entire group to review and discuss the experiences of the weekend, with particular emphasis on ways participants can apply what they have learned to the groups they will lead. Time is allowed for debriefing and for talking about the meaning this workshop had for each person.

In conducting a didactic and experiential workshop to develop group leadership skills, several cautions must be kept in mind. It is difficult to combine a skills development and cognitive framework of group process with personal involvement for therapeutic purposes. Both the students and the supervisors/instructors need to remind themselves that the workshop has a dual purpose. One aim of the workshop is a *didactic* or teaching focus on learning how groups function, learning about group dynamics, and acquiring specific skills necessary to lead groups effectively. The other aim is to provide a climate of support and challenge that encourages students to get personally involved sufficiently to acquire some tools to continue taking an honest look at themselves as persons and to assess how their personal characteristics might either facilitate or inhibit their ability to lead groups.

There are two tendencies that might occur in such a workshop. On one extreme, the focus can be directed toward acquiring cognitive knowledge, skills, and techniques. A problem with this extreme is that if the personal investment of dealing with real issues is lacking, then the group becomes artificial. If the group is characterized by artificiality, any meaningful learning of leadership skills and techniques becomes difficult. On the other extreme is the tendency to forget matters of group process and the learning and practicing of skills and to become simply an "experiential group."

We take care to combine both the experiential and didactic dimensions, based on our conviction that such a balance is essential for learning how to lead groups. However emotionally intense the groups may become, we do not abandon the educational aspects. Participants can be involved in personal self-exploration and still put their learnings into a cognitive framework. The focus on exploring their own struggles stems from our assumption that leaders cannot inspire others to do what they are not willing to do themselves.

Our experience in doing training workshops has shown us that the participants learn best when the material arises from what they actually experience in a session. This kind on ongoing teaching/learning process seems to have an impact on students: what they are conceptualizing has its roots in a problem they have actually faced as either a member or a leader of their training group.

PROCESS PAPER FOR THE WEEKEND WORKSHOP

For this three-day weekend workshop described above, students enroll in the course Human Services 416 (*Group Process and Membership*) for one semester unit of credit. The course does not carry a letter grade, but is evaluated simply as "Credit" or "No Credit." This removes the evaluative component of this kind of experiential group training. Students are not given a grade for their performance in the workshop—neither as a group member nor as a group leader. To obtain credit, students are required to attend all of the sessions for the weekend (about 24 contact hours) and also to write a thoughtful reflection paper that conceptualizes their learnings based on the weekend group experience. Below are the directions to students for this written assignment.

To obtain credit for Huser 416 (*Group Process and Membership*) a paper dealing with both your personal learnings and group process learnings is due the third week of class. This paper will not receive a letter grade, but will be evaluated on the basis of satisfactory or unsatisfactory. To receive credit for the one unit Huser 416 course, it is necessary to attend the pre-workshop orientation meeting, to attend all the sessions of the three-day weekend workshop, and to complete a satisfactory paper in a timely manner. This paper should be about **12 pages.** It should reflect a conceptualization of your learnings from the weekend workshop, and is to reflect the application of both the books *Groups: Process and Practice* and also *Group Techniques* to your weekend workshop. You are asked to focus on stages of group, techniques and practice, and group process concepts and the evolution of the group process. Apply your readings to an analysis of your own experience in the workshop group. Do a process commentary from the perspective of both a group leader and a group member. Do not give a report of events, but do write about key group process issues that unfolded in your group. Please don't be riveted to the guidelines given below in writing about your learnings and experience in the workshop. The main point is to write a comprehensive, honest, and clear report on what you learned and how you learned it. Focus on conceptualizing the themes of the workshop experience. Avoid mentioning others in the group by name on all of your papers. Below are some guidelines that will hopefully be useful in structuring your paper.

- What did you learn about yourself through this process?

- Focus on the qualities about yourself that might either enhance or detract from your effectiveness as a group leader.

- Concretely, what did this workshop teach you about being a group member? about group leadership? about *how* groups function or malfunction? about the stages of a group? about techniques?

- Comment on the evolution and development of your supervision group on the weekend. How did your group begin and end? Any key transitions? Any turning points? Any highlights in your group?
- How did the presence of the supervisor effect your group? How did the rotation of student co-leaders from session to session effect your group?
- What group norms developed? How were these norms shaped? Were these norms explicit or implicit?
- Comment on the level of cohesion in your group.
- What did you learn about techniques and skills at this weekend supervision and training workshop?
- What factors contribute to a working and productive group?
- How is trust generated within a group?
- When do groups get stuck, and how can they get unstuck?
- How is resistance best dealt with in groups? How about anxiety?
- How is conflict therapeutically dealt with in groups?
- What have you learned about groups from this workshop that you can apply to groups that you'll lead during this semester?

PART III
Guidelines and Suggestions for Chapters

Learning Objectives, Key Terms, Lecture Outlines, Focus Questions, T-F and Multiple-Choice Quizzes

CHAPTER 1 INTRODUCTION TO GROUP WORK

Lecture Notes and Outline for the Chapter

I. *Learning Objectives.* It is expected that the students will demonstrate a basic understanding of:

A. The distinctions among the various stages of groups;

B. The rationale for group counseling;

C. The unique values of group counseling for special populations;

D. The purposes of structured groups and special strategies in designing structured group experiences;

E. The factors that lead to the increase of self-help groups, and the differences between the self-help group and the therapy group; and

F. The role that social and cultural factors play in the group-counseling process, including a grasp of the following issues pertaining to group counseling in a multicultural context: the trend toward multicultural awareness, the challenges and rewards of group work with various cultures, general guidelines for work with multicultural populations, methods of preparing clients for group experience, and learning to become a culturally effective group counselor.

II. *Key Terms to Define, Describe, and Explain*

- group counseling
- group psychotherapy
- support groups
- structured groups
- self-help groups
- social microcosm
- task groups
- multicultural counseling
- race
- ethnicity
- minority group
- cultural encapsulation
- psychoeducation group

III. *Lecture Outline: Notes and Comments*

In this chapter my basic attempt is to provide an overview for the students of the entire course. For the details of the first session, which includes material from this chapter, I refer you to the course outline that I provide elsewhere in this manual.

Focus Questions for Chapter 1: Introduction to Group Work

The following questions can be useful to focus students on key concepts in studying as well as to provide a guide for class discussions. They can also be used as the basis for written examinations or for take-home papers.

1. Define group counseling. What are some specific goals of group counseling?

2. Provide a rationale for group counseling. Include the major values of group counseling.

3. What are some of the advantages of the values of group counseling with the following populations?
   a. groups for children
   b. groups for adolescents
   c. groups for college students
   d. groups for the elderly

4. Define group psychotherapy. What are some of the basic differences between group counseling and group psychotherapy with respect to goals, format, structure, process, and focus?

5. Define and describe an example of a structured group. What is the main purpose of such a group? What are some of the reasons that structured groups are increasingly finding a place in many settings? How can structured groups be aimed at education of a particular population, as well as providing opportunities for members to engage in personal sharing and self-exploration?

6. What is the difference between self-help groups and a therapy group? Describe what a typical self-help group might be like, including how it differs from other kinds of groups. What are your thoughts regarding the future of self-help groups?

7. Mention what you consider to be a value of the self-help group. Do you see any particular advantages of self-help groups over professionally led groups? Are there any dangers or limitations of self-help groups?

8. What is the importance of considering the cultural backgrounds of both the members and the leader in designing and facilitating counseling groups in a multicultural context? What are some of the dangers of making stereotyped generalizations about individuals within a particular social or cultural group? How might group counselors encounter resistance from some ethnic or minority clients because they are using traditional White, middle-class values as the basis for facilitating a group? What are some ways to avoid becoming a culturally encapsulated group counselor?

9. What are some particular advantages of using groups with multicultural populations? What are some limitations and cautions in using group work in a multicultural context?

10. Describe some general guidelines that you might employ as a group practitioner in working with culturally diverse populations. How might you prepare the members for a successful group experience? How might you acquire the personal characteristics that are required for becoming a culturally effective group counselor?

CHAPTER 2   GROUP LEADERSHIP

Lecture Notes and Outline for the Chapter

I. *Learning Objectives.* After reading and studying this chapter, the students are expected to have a basic understanding of problems and issues facing them as group leaders, the skills and techniques of leadership at various stages of a group, and an awareness of the skills and functions needed for effective group leading. Specific learning objectives include:

   A. An awareness of their own personal characteristics and how these are related to group leadership;

   B. A familiarization with the basic problems and issues that face beginning group leaders as well as a clarification of their position on how to deal with matters such as anxiety, self-disclosure, and co-leading groups;

   C. Opportunities to practice basic intervention and group leadership skills;

   D. A recognition of the importance of developing one's own unique style of group leadership;

   E. A basic grasp of the skills and some techniques in opening and closing group sessions;

   F. An understanding of the special challenges of doing group work in an institutional setting;

   G. Identifying specific beliefs and attitudes, knowledge, and skills that are essential in becoming a culturally skilled group counselor; and

   H. An understanding of the importance of the group leader's willingness to adapt his or her techniques to the multicultural context of group work.

II. *Lecture Outline: Notes and Comments*

   A. Introduction
      1. Although we focus on the topic of the group leader at this point in the course, we will come back to this topic during the entire course. Issues come up as the students are leading groups and thus cannot be covered in one week allocated to the subject.

   B. The Group Leader as a Person
      1. My bias is to emphasize that group leaders will be no more effective as leaders than they are as human beings. Thus, we focus on personal characteristics that may be facilitative or inhibitory in a group.
      2. The text identifies the following personal characteristics as being most important as variables related to effective group leadership: presence, personal power, courage, willingness to

confront oneself, sincerity and authenticity, sense of identity, belief in group process and enthusiasm, and inventiveness and creativity. A good discussion catalyst is to ask students to identify what they consider to be the few most important personal characteristics of the effective group counselor.
   3. In their own self-directed groups, these students are expected to look honestly at their own level of courage, their degree of genuineness, their own sense of enthusiasm, and so on. I believe that their willingness to continually look at themselves and to work on their own struggles should be given priority. During the course, they can continually take opportunities to deal with their own feelings, values, and conflicts as these surface in the work they do as beginning group leaders.
C. Problems and Issues Facing Group Leaders
   1. An excellent way to provide the focus on the leader as a person is to begin with questions such as: What are your motivations for wanting to be a group leader? What personal needs are met through leading groups? How do you grow personally from the interactions you have with the members of your group and with your co-leader? How do you deal with the anxieties that you face as a group leader?
   2. The *Student Manual* has a number of suggestions for activities in class, including role-playing possibilities.
   3. We spend much time on matters dealing with working effectively with co-leaders. This includes discussing what members can learn through the modeling done by co-leaders.
D. Overview of Techniques and Therapeutic Interventions: Skills and Functions of Group Leaders
   1. I expect students to be able to identify, define, describe, and give clear examples of the basic skills and functions of group leaders. These terms and skills are:
      - active listening
      - restating
      - clarifying
      - summarizing
      - questioning
      - interpreting
      - confronting
      - reflecting feelings
      - supporting
      - empathizing
      - facilitating
      - initiating
      - goal setting
      - evaluating
      - giving feedback
      - suggesting
      - protecting
      - disclosing oneself
      - modeling
      - linking
      - blocking
      - terminating
   2. In my lectures on group leadership skills I give a brief description of each skill and often demonstrate this skill in the classroom. I've often had the students follow by working on this skill in triads. For instance, if the skill being taught is *ques-*

tioning, I'll ask students to mention what some problems might be with the overuse of questions. I'll make a few observations, demonstrate the skill, and provide opportunities for them to practice asking open-ended (as opposed to closed-type) questions.
3. I find trouble in attempting to teach each skill in a systematic and isolated manner. Although I do spend time in going through each skill, I prefer to teach these skills in a more indirect manner at the weekend workshops and in the experiential groups in class.
4. The list of specific skills and functions provides a framework for ongoing evaluation of the group leaders. In the *Student Manual* you'll see a 22-item evaluation form, which contains the 22 skills listed here plus other specific leadership skills. I have evaluated the leaders on this scale when I have observed their group leading directly. I use this form as one basis for a private discussion with the student to talk about progress in learning and mastering the skills. Even more important is the leader's *self-evaluation*. Students are asked to complete this evaluation at three points during the semester; their co-leader also completes the evaluation. In this way the students have feedback from several sources.

E. Skills in Opening and Closing Group Sessions
1. The *Student Manual* contains some guidelines that students have found helpful in opening and closing a particular group session. I find that students need practice and coaching in these skills; too often there is very little effort made to tie one session to another.
2. Consult the *Student Manual* for specific exercises that you might find useful in group work related to opening and closing in addition to a detailed list of questions as a review/checklist for examining one's level of skill development on the 22 skills described.

F. Developing Your Style of Group Leadership
1. Students generally find this a topic of interest. You might consider giving a lecture on the various styles of group leadership, and then asking students to form smaller groups to clarify which style comes closest to their own.
2. A problem that may occur is that the beginning student in group counseling most likely has little feel for "a style of leadership." My attempt is to get them thinking about what style they might develop.

Focus Questions for Chapter 2: Group Leadership

1. What are the personal characteristics that you deem most essential for effective group leadership? What are some personal assets you possess that you think will be of assistance to you as a group leader?

2. Anxiety is frequently experienced by beginning group leaders. Discuss how you might experience anxiety when you think about being involved in the work of group leading.

3. What are the major concerns you have when you think about becoming a group leader? Discuss what you consider to be one of your most pressing concerns.

4. Self-disclosure is both a skill and a process that group leaders need to learn. What guidelines can you develop to assist you in determining whether or not your disclosures are facilitative? What kinds of problems do you anticipate, if any, in the area of self-disclosure as a group leader?

5. After reviewing the specific group-leadership skills in the textbook and the *Student Manual*, identify the skills you think are your areas of strength. Which skills do you see as needing the most improvement? How might you go about developing these skills?

6. Special skills are needed to effectively open and close each group session. Mention a few procedures you might employ on a routine basis as a way to open and to close.

7. What do you see as being the main advantages of working with a co-leader? What about some disadvantages?

*8. What are some specific characteristics that you'd most look for in selecting a co-leader? Explain why you selected these factors. Mention some things you would want to discuss with your co-leader before you approached a new group.

9. Assume that you are working in an institutional setting (a state mental hospital) and you have developed a plan for organizing and leading a weekly group for some of the patients. What obstacles might you encounter as you seek to get your program approved and implemented within the system? Discuss ways you could deal with these frustrations.

10. Mention and discuss what you see as being the most significant forces that have affected your style of group leading.

NOTE: In the *Student Manual* there is a checklist of guidelines for meeting with a co-leader. I suggest looking over these 15 guidelines as a concrete way of identifying the areas where students see themselves functioning especially well and those areas needing improvement. These guidelines can be productively used by having co-leaders ask each other relevant questions as they process their relationship throughout the course of a group's history.

Evaluation Form for Group Leaders

In the *Student Manual* I've provided a 22-item assessment form of the specific skills that are discussed in the textbook, along with a checklist of questions that can help leaders focus on their level of skill development on these various dimensions. The form that follows is somewhat similar for the first 22 items (without the self-examination questions), yet it has additional items.

I use this particular form at least three times during the semester. I ask the leaders to fill out the self-inventory form for themselves, and I also ask that the co-leaders rate each other. In personal conferences with the students (which I often hold with the co-leader pairs), these self-inventory forms can be used as a basis for specific discussion of areas needing particular improvement.

If this evaluation form appears to be something that would be of use to you and your students, you can have it reproduced and use it in addition to the shorter form that is in the *Student Manual*. If you directly supervise your students, then you might use this form as an evaluation device.

Evaluation Form of Group Leader Skills

The following evaluation form can be used in several ways. It can be used by group leaders as a self-evaluation form, which is its basic purpose. This self-inventory will give you, as group leaders, a set of criteria to assess many of your strengths and specific areas that need improvement. This form can also be used by co-leaders to rate each other, by supervisors to evaluate leadership performance, and by group members as a basis of evaluating their leaders.

The following specific variables are to be rated on a five-point scale, using the following code.

 5 = This is done almost always with an exceptional degree of competence.
 4 = This is done much of the time with a high degree of competence.
 3 = This is done sometimes with an adequate degree of competence.
 2 = This is done occasionally with a relatively low level of competence.
 1 = This is rarely demonstrated, or done with an extremely low level of competence.

NOTE: Above, all, strive for the maximum degree of honesty with yourself as you complete this rating scale.

To what degree does the group leader demonstrate:

____ 1. *active listening* (the ability to hear, understand, and communicate this understanding)?

____ 2. *restating* (the ability to capture the essence of what is said in different words with the effect of adding meaning or clarifying meaning)?

____ 3. *clarifying* (focusing on underlying issues and assisting others in getting a clearer picture of what they are thinking and feeling)?

_____ 4. *summarizing* (being able to tie together loose ends, identify common themes, and provide a picture of the directional trends of a group session)?

_____ 5. *questioning* (the ability to use questions to stimulate thought and action, and to avoid a question/answer pattern of interaction between the leader and members)?

_____ 6. *interpretation* (explaining the meaning of behavior patterns within the framework of a theoretical system)?

_____ 7. *confrontation* (the ability to challenge members in a direct way on discrepancies in such a manner that they will tend to react nondefensively to the confrontation)?

_____ 8. *reflecting feelings* (mirroring what others appear to be feeling without being mechanical)?

_____ 9. *supporting* (being able to offer some form of positive reinforcement at appropriate times in such a way that it has a facilitating effect)?

_____ 10. *empathy* (intuitively sensing the subjective world of others in a group, being able to adopt the frame of reference of others, and communicating this understanding to clients so that they feel understood)?

_____ 11. *facilitating* (the ability to help members to clarify their own goals and take the steps to reach them)?

_____ 12. *initiating* (demonstrating an active stance in intervening in a group at appropriate times)?

_____ 13. *goal setting* (being able to cooperatively work with members so that there is an alignment between member goals and leader goals, and being able to assist members in establishing concrete goals)?

_____ 14. *feedback* (giving information to members in such a way that they can use it to make constructive behavior changes)?

_____ 15. *suggestion* (offering information or possibilities for action that can be used by members in making independent decisions)?

_____ 16. *protecting* (the willingness to actively intervene to ensure that members will be safeguarded from unnecessary psychological risks)?

_____ 17. *self-disclosure* (demonstrating the ability and willingness to share persistent reactions with the members that relate to the here-and-now occurrences in the group)?

_____ 18. *modeling* (demonstrating to members desired behaviors that can be practiced both during and after group sessions)?

_____ 19. *silence* (the ability to effectively deal with the meaning underlying silence in a group session)?

_____ 20. *blocking* (being able to intervene effectively without attacking members who engage in counterproductive behaviors in group)?

_____ 21. *terminating* (creating a climate that encourages members to continue working after sessions)?

_____ 22. *assignment* (suggesting to clients specific activities that they can practice both in and out of group to develop new behaviors)?

_____ 23. *role direction* (being able to direct members to enact specific roles in role-playing situations)?

_____ 24. *diagnosing* (the ability to assess specific problems or conflicts of members in such a way that avoids labeling them)?

_____ 25. *evaluating* (the ongoing appraisal of the process and outcomes of a group)?

_____ 26. *following through* (the ability to implement and follow through to reasonable completion work that is begun with a client)?

_____ 27. *knowledge of theory* (demonstrating a theoretical understanding of group dynamics, interpersonal dynamics, and drawing on a model or models in group leading)?

_____ 28. *application of theory to practice* (the skill in applying theoretical constructs to actual group practice)?

_____ 29. *perceptivity and insight* (sensitively and accurately seeing underlying issues and getting at the core of both verbal and nonverbal communications)?

_____ 30. *referral* (presenting to members resources for continued personal growth in such a way that they are likely to seriously consider using these resources)?

_____ 31. *risk-taking* (the willingness to risk making mistakes and an openness in learning from them)?

_____ 32. *inventiveness and creativity* (being able to approach a group with fresh ideas, and being able to synthesize a personal therapeutic style from a variety of therapeutic approaches)?

_____ 33. *enthusiasm* (a sense of aliveness, a belief in group process, and the ability to influence members' level of excitement)?

_____ 34. *expression* (being able to verbally express thought and feelings in an effective manner)?

_____ 35. *awareness of self* (being aware of personal needs, motivations, problems, values, and the impact they have on group process)?

_____ 36. *group dynamics* (being aware of the many levels of interaction in a group and assisting members in working effectively together)?

_____ 37. *content orientation* (helping members to focus on certain themes in a structured type of group)?

_____ 38. *cooperation as a co-leader* (the ability to effectively work with a co-leader, to plan together, and the ability to carry out these plans in a group)?

_____ 39. *values awareness* (awareness of how leader's values can either facilitate or inhibit the functioning of a group, and the ability to expose leader values without imposing them on members)?

_____ 40. *ethical awareness* (demonstrating a knowledge and sensitivity to the demands of the professional responsibility of leading a group)?

_____ 41. *techniques* (knowing a range of techniques or therapeutic procedures and being able to use them appropriately in helping members work through personal issues)?

_____ 42. *flexibility* (the willingness to change an agenda, modify a structure, change strategies, and in other ways adapt to the unique needs of a particular member or a certain group)?

_____ 43. *psychological presence* (the ability to be emotionally in contact with members, and being psychologically ready to lead a particular session)?

_____ 44. *genuineness* (being what one is, the absence of false fronts, a congruence between inner experiencing and external expression, avoiding hiding in roles)?

_____ 45. *structuring* (the ability to use appropriate structuring in a group so that members do not become leader dependent but at the same time do not flounder needlessly)?

_____ 46. *belief in group process* (demonstrating a belief in the values of a group for influencing constructive changes)?

_____ 47. *personal power* (using personal power in such a way that members are not encouraged to adopt a dependent or inferior position)?

_____ 48. *respect* (communicating an attitude of acceptance and seeing value in others and valuing the dignity and autonomy of the members)?

_____ 49. *care* (experiencing and demonstrating an attitude of genuine caring, warmth, and concern for the members)?

_____ 50. *courage* (demonstrating the willingness to do for oneself what is expected of members and being willing to face oneself honestly)?

Some Suggestions for Using This Inventory

1. Go back over the preceding skills and functions and review your list.

2. What did you learn about yourself from thinking about these questions and applying them to yourself?

3. List some of the specific areas (such as "active listening," "interpreting," "questions," and so on) that you think will give you the *most* difficulty as a group leader.

CHAPTER 3   ETHICAL AND PROFESSIONAL ISSUES IN GROUP PRACTICE

Lecture Notes and Outline for the Chapter
  I. *Learning Objectives*
     A. To familiarize students with *the Professional Standards for Training of Group Workers* (of the ASGW, 1991);
     B. To challenge students to develop their own ethical and professional standards, and to provide them with the tools needed to interpret and translate general ethical guidelines into appropriate and specific principles that will govern their practice; and

C. To raise issues and cases that deal with the ethics of group work, such as: the rights of group participants, informed consent, voluntary participation, freedom of exit, the right to confidentiality, psychological risks in groups, the ethics of the group leader's actions, the impact of the leader's values on the group, uses and misuses of group techniques, legal liability and malpractice, the group leader's competence, perspectives on training group counselors, and suggestions for developing an ethical and professional orientation to group work.

II. *Lecture Outline: Notes and Comments*
   A. Introduction and basic approach to exploring ethical issues
      1. Rather than using a lecture approach, I've found that discussion of cases and situations increases student involvement.
      2. Having students form small subgroups to discuss ethical issues in group work is a useful way to facilitate a questioning stance. In these small groups, the students can also share their answers to the self-inventories and specific cases given in the student manual for this chapter. These self-assessment devices include:
         a. a self-inventory to assess views on ethical practice in group work;
         b. exercises and activities (short vignettes of group situations); and
         c. a self-inventory to evaluate ethical decision-making and a review of basic issues.

Focus Questions for Chapter 3: Ethical and Professional Issues in Group Practice

1. What are the rights of group participants? What rights do you think are most important to explore with potential members before they enter a group and soon after they join a group?

2. Informed consent is seen as a basic right of those who enter a group. What type of information would you want to provide to clients before they join one of your groups? What are some of the ways you might help members to understand both their rights and responsibilities as group members?

3. What ethical issues do you think are involved in leading groups composed of involuntary members? Do you see any differences in ethical issues with groups of involuntary clients versus voluntary clients?

4. What are your thoughts on a member's right to leave a group? What would you want to tell members of your group about your policies on leaving a group?

5. At times, groups involve coercion and undue pressure. Although some degree of group pressure is inevitable, what measures would you want

to take to lessen the chances of inappropriate pressure upon group members?

6. What are some ethical issues related to multicultural group counseling?

7. What do you see as your responsibility as a group leader to help members get their fair share of group time? How might you help them to make maximum use of the resources within the group?

8. Confidentiality is a central ethical issue in group counseling. What are some of the specific issues that you would want to raise with group members during the early stage of a group? How would you explain the purposes and parameters of confidentiality?

9. What would you tell your members about the exceptions to confidentiality?

10. There are certain psychological risks involved in participating in a group. What do you consider to be some of the major risks of being in a group? As a group leader, what is your role in minimizing these psychological risks?

11. On the matter of socializing among group members outside of the group sessions, what would you want to tell the participants? What are some potential advantages and disadvantages of socializing among group members?

12. What are your thoughts about the ethical issues of group leaders forming personal or social relationships with members in their group? What about making social contacts once members have terminated such a group?

13. What do you see as the role that your values play on the group process? Do you have any thoughts on how you might expose your values without imposing them on the group members? What are some situations where you might expect difficulties because of a conflict between your values and the values of a particular group member?

14. What ethical issues are involved in the appropriate use of group techniques? What are some possible misuses of group techniques?

15. Given the fact that mental health practitioners are more vulnerable to a malpractice suit, what are some of your thoughts about the ways you might lessen the chances of your being sued as a group leader? What do you see as some of the potential issues pertaining to legal liability? How might a group practitioner be vulnerable to legal action?

16. What aspects of your education and training have you valued the most with respect to preparing you for effectively leading groups? What kinds of experiences do you think would have been beneficial to preparing you for group leadership? Review the ASGW's "Professional Standards for Training of Group Workers." Assuming that you plan to lead groups as a part of your professional work, assess your current

level of competence in the areas of knowledge, skill, and clinical practice. What steps can you take in order to add to your experience?

17. The textbook discusses perspectives on training group counselors. What are your thoughts about the essential components of a program designed to train effective group counselors? What are your thoughts on requiring, or strongly encouraging, participation in a therapeutic group as a part of a training program for group counselors?

18. If you were invited to be a participant on a board for establishing continuing education recommendations for group practitioners, what ideas would you want to bring to this board? What kind of knowledge and skills would you deem most important as a part of maintaining confidence as a group counselor?

19. What are some specific ethical issues that you see as being most important during each of the stages of a group? What considerations do you think are important before the group begins? Mention some ethical considerations during the early stages of a group's development. Identify a few ethical considerations during the later stages of a group's development. What are some issues to consider after the termination of a group?

20. What are some of your ideas regarding ways of developing an ethical and professional orientation to group work? Mention some of your thoughts about procedures you might use in dealing with ethical dilemmas you might encounter as a group counselor.

CHAPTER 4   EARLY STAGES IN THE DEVELOPMENT OF A GROUP

Lecture Notes and Outline for the Chapter
I. *Learning Objectives.* Some examples of specific learning objectives related to the early stages of a group's development are as follows:

A. To become familiar with issues involved in forming a group;

B. To learn the major tasks of the group leader during the early stages in group development;

C. To become aware of the characteristics of groups during the early stages and the unique tasks of the group so that appropriate interventions can be made;

D. To recognize common problems of groups during the early stages as well as to develop ideas for constructively dealing with these conflicts and problems;

E. To learn the basics of group process, especially as these group-process concepts apply to the early stages;

F. To have a grasp of ways to best prepare members for a group, including ways of teaching members how to profit from a group;

G. To have an understanding of important issues that co-leaders need to discuss during the early stages of a group; and

H. To acquire a clear understanding of the nature of resistance as well as methods of dealing constructively with the forms of resistance and for dealing with difficult group members.

II. *Key Terms to Identify and Define*
- homogeneous group
- heterogeneous group
- open group
- closed group
- orientation and exploration stage
- modeling
- division of responsibility
- structuring
- transition stage
- resistance

III. *Lecture Outline: Notes and Comments*
   A. Pregroup Issues: Formation of the Group
      1. I tend to give emphasis to the pregroup phase, as it is critical that students realize the importance of a solid job of preparing both themselves as leaders and the group members to increase the chances of successful outcomes.
      2. Often I have the students write and present in small groups a proposal for a group that they will be leading or co-leading. Guidelines for such a proposal are found in the *Student Manual* for Chapter 4.
      3. Typically, we'll do some experiential work with matters such as screening interviews, ways of selecting group members, and dealing with the practical concerns in the formation of a group. We devote a good deal of time to ways of preparing group members for a group experience, and for teaching these members the basics of group process.

   B. Stage I: Orientation and Exploration Stage
      1. During the initial meetings of this class on group counseling we focus on building trust as a learning community. I tend to do a lot of work in dyads and triads so that people get acquainted. We talk about the trust level needed for effective learning in this course.

   C. Stage II: Transition Stage
      1. I stress that these stages are merely descriptive and provide a conceptual framework for understanding the evolution of a group. At times students tend to think in concrete and rigid terms, and expect to see clear lines between these stages in the groups they lead.
      2. We go into depth on the characteristics of the transition stage, including extended discussions on the role of factors such as the

following in groups: anxiety, defensiveness, resistance, the struggle for control, conflict, and challenging the authority of the group leader.
   3. Sometimes students see anxiety, resistance, and conflict as "something to get around" or as negative signs in a group. I attempt to develop a respect for these variables, and I stress the importance of recognizing and fully dealing with these factors when they arise in a group. One of the best ways I've found to deal with such matters is to deal with the anxieties and resistances that become evident in the students who are taking the group counseling course. Thus, we deal directly with the anxiety of "doing well as a group leader."
D. Resistance
   1. One of the central aspects of group process that I focus on in my group leadership course is the nature of resistance, along with methods of recognizing and dealing constructively with this phenomenon. My preference is to have students look at their own resistance as evidenced by fears of making mistakes, ambivalence over wanting it to remain comfortable versus taking the risks involved in knowing themselves more deeply, and other manifestations of avoidance in terms of dealing with themselves personally.
E. Forms of Resistant Behavior in Group Members
   1. As mentioned above, I attempt to focus on the resistance that the students might experience. In keeping with this focus, when we deal with the types of problem behaviors in group members (such as monopolistic behavior, silence, and avoidance), an attempt is made to have the group leaders focus on their *own* dynamics, not merely the problem behaviors of the members.
   2. This can be done by asking students to explore in small groups topics such as: What kinds of members do you find yourself having the strongest reactions toward? How do certain "problem members" activate your own unfinished business, feelings of inadequacy, or feelings of competitiveness?
   3. Rather than categorizing "problem members," my preference is to deal with behaviors that people *sometimes* show in groups. This avoids reducing a participant to a simplistic label, and it lessens the chances of having members live up to predetermined categories.

Some Suggested Exercises and Activities for Chapter 4

In addition to the exercises provided in the manual, the following are some other activities that you might want to suggest to your students as a basis for small-group discussion and interaction.

1. You might encourage your students to really experiment with ideas for groups. I've found that students frequently censor many creative ideas based on fears that these ideas might be perceived as "dumb." I often ask students to explore their fears in designing a proposal for a group.

   Such questions as the following might be useful catalysts.
   - What are your fears concerning what might happen to your group proposal? What fears do you have concerning how people might respond when you present your proposal for a group?
   - What would you hope for when you present the idea for a group?

2. Suggest to your class that they assume the identity of a community group. One or two students can then present a proposal to this "community group" (or school board). The audience can ask questions of the students who presented the proposal, much like they would imagine a community group might respond. After the proposal has been presented, and the "community group" has asked questions, feedback should be given to the people who presented their proposal. This is a useful way to refine a proposal before actually presenting it to a certain group.

3. You might want to give your students practice in thinking about ways they would announce a group and recruit members. I've introduced this topic in my classes by saying something like: "Announcing a group can be touchy. If your group was something you believed in strongly, how would you announce it to potential members? What would you say in written and verbal announcements?"

4. Typically, I'll have the class do some type *of screening-interview exercise.* (See the *Student Manual* for a sample of this exercise.) I usually do not tell them what questions to ask. After they have done a few interviews, I'll then suggest some questions that they might have overlooked. Some of these questions that I ask students to consider in doing private interviews include:
   - Why are you applying for this group?
   - What do you most hope you'll get from the group?
   - What have you heard about groups?
   - What are some of your concerns that you'd be willing to explore in a group?
   - What expectations do you have of the group leader?
   - Do you have any fears or reservations about joining this group?
   - What are you willing to do to achieve your goals in this group?
   - How willing are you to invest yourself in a personal way in the group?
   - Do you have any questions that you'd like to ask concerning this group?

5. You might consider exploring some of these questions with your class. I often have the students work with questions such as the following in small discussion groups, as I move from one group to the next.
   - What functions and tasks do you see as most important for you as a group leader before a group actually begins? What pre-group issues and concerns do you think are most pressing?
   - How would you take care of the matter of introductions? Brainstorm some ways of having members introduce themselves in a new group. How would you introduce yourself? As a leader, what would you say about yourself to a group that you were meeting for the first time?
   - Discuss the pros and cons of conducting screening interviews for groups.

6. The focus questions for Chapter 4 can serve as excellent catalyst questions for small group interaction. I find it useful to work in small groups, as well as in an entire class. These focus questions are ones that I've discovered to be of value in getting my students to think about group process and to bring their ideas to the entire class. Typically, I'll give the groups a specific set of questions to explore, and I'll ask that each group elect a set of co-leaders (to serve as discussion leaders or group facilitators of certain exercises and as recorders). After a designated time, all the groups meet as an entire class, and each group has the recorder give a brief summary of the group proceedings.

7. In this chapter my central emphasis is on methods of creating trust in a group. One of the best ways of establishing trust is to deal with the fears of members, their reservations, or any sense of lack of trust and to deal with resistances. The following two exercises are ones that I use in conjunction with the issue of creating a trusting climate in a group.

8. The following exercise can be used as a way of getting acquainted in a newly formed group. In your group or class, break into dyads. Every five to ten minutes select a new partner and discuss a different issue each time. Some of these issues might be:
   - What reservations do you have about groups?
   - What do you fear about groups?
   - How do you imagine it would be for you to co-lead with the person who is your current partner?

9. What would you do as a leader if, despite your best attempts, your group seemed to be marked by distrust? For example, you could pick a group member and ask that person what he or she imagines would happen if he or she were to disclose the things that were personally significant. You could ask each member to complete the sentence: "If I were to trust you. . . ." or "I don't trust you because. . . ." You could model by telling members how you feel in this group. Or, you might consider disbanding the group. What other courses of action can you think of for a group that doesn't develop trust?

Focus Questions for Chapter 4: Early Stages in the Development of a Group

Questions on Pregroup Issues
1. If you were to announce a group you were developing, what items would you include? What would you say in your announcement that would give prospective group members a clear idea about what they might expect from the group?
2. What are your thoughts concerning the screening of group members? In screening and selecting members, what criteria would you use, and what would you be looking for?
3. What are some specific questions that you would ask of the potential group members in a screening interview?
4. If you were developing a group, what would you keep in mind regarding the composition of the group? Consider such factors as age, sex, common problems, and membership characteristics.
5. What kind of preparation do you see as useful for group members? If you were to lead a group, what are some specific areas you might cover as a basis for preparing members for a successful group?

The Orientation and Exploration Phase of a Group
6. What are the major characteristics of the initial stage of a group? A major task of this stage is that of inclusion and identity. What do you see as your role in helping the members successfully deal with this task?
7. What are some specific steps that you would take as a group leader in creating trust within the group? What role do you see the leader as playing in modeling behavior that will lead to trust?

The Transition Stage of a Group
8. How is conflict a major characteristic of the transition stage of a group?
9. How do you view defensiveness and resistance in a group? Discuss how these characteristics are a part of the transition stage.
10. What are the positive meanings of the situations in which group members challenge the leader? How might this be an important turning point in a group? In what way could this be related to a group's movement toward autonomy?
11. Discuss the concept of resistance as something that is typical of most group members. How can this resistance be recognized and dealt with effectively?
12. If you had a group member who habitually said very little, what might you do? What are the possible reasons for nonparticipating behavior?

13. In what way do you see the member who tends to monopolize the time of a group as employing resistive behavior? What ideas do you have concerning how you think you'd deal with this type of behavior in a group?

14. What kind of resistive behavior in group members do you think you'd have the greatest difficulty in dealing with? Discuss how you might deal with your own feelings and reactions generated by the member who displays this kind of behavior.

CHAPTER 5 LATER STAGES IN THE DEVELOPMENT OF A GROUP

Lecture Notes and Outline for the Chapter

I. *Learning Objectives.* Some examples of specific learning objectives related to the later stages of a group's development are as follows:

   A. To learn the major tasks of the group leader during the later stages in the development of a group;

   B. To become aware of the characteristics of groups during the later stages and the unique tasks of the group so that appropriate interventions can be made;

   C. To recognize common problems of groups during the later stages as well as to develop ideas for constructively dealing with these conflicts and problems;

   D. To learn the basics of group process, especially as these group-process concepts apply to the later stages;

   E. To learn effective ways of terminating a group;

   F. To become familiar with issues involved in follow-up evaluation procedures; and

   G. To have an understanding of important issues that co-leaders need to discuss during the later stages of a group.

II. *Key Terms to Identify and Define*
   - working stage
   - group cohesion
   - catharsis
   - cognitive restructuring
   - therapeutic factors
   - feedback
   - self-disclosure
   - confrontation
   - consolidation of learnings

III. *Lecture Outline: Notes and Comments*

   A. Stage III: Working Stage
      1. Since group cohesion is such a critical factor in group work, we explore this concept in depth with stress on how to recognize it and ways of developing cohesion in groups.

2. Students take the list of characteristics of an effective group that are listed in the textbook and apply it to the groups they are working with. We also apply these characteristics to our own classroom group. This makes the characteristics more of a reality.
  B. Stage IV: Consolidation and Termination
    1. I find that students in training often deal poorly with matters of separation and termination. At the beginning of the course we discuss effective ways of terminating groups, then we come back to this phase toward the end of the course for more detailed treatment. As the groups students are leading are coming to an end, we stress key aspects to look for as well as procedures for increasing the chances of transfer of learning from the group to everyday life.
  C. Postgroup Issues: Follow-up and Evaluation Procedures
    1. I encourage students who are leading groups as a part of the course requirement to meet on an individual basis with the members of their group. In class, we discuss specifics to explore in this postgroup interview.
    2. Also, I ask the group leaders to develop some form for ongoing feedback and evaluation so that they can evaluate their effectiveness as leaders. This is also done in the class itself.

Focus Questions for Chapter 5: Later Stages in the Development of a Group

The Working Stage of a Group
1. Discuss how the development of cohesion is a central characteristic of the working stage of a group. What is your understanding of "group cohesion"? What factors lead to this unity in a group?
2. List and briefly describe what you consider to be the major characteristics of an effective and working group. What do you see as being the basic differences between a productive and a nonproductive group?
3. Discuss what you consider to be the role and tasks of the group leader during the working stage.
4. Discuss the ways in which you and your co-leader might go about evaluating the direction and productivity of your group as it reaches the working stage. How would you encourage the group members to do their own evaluating at this point?

The Consolidation Stage of a Group
5. Imagine that you and your co-leader are meeting to discuss the termination of your group, which is three weeks away. What issues are most important to focus on during this stage?

6. What are some specific steps and procedures for assisting group members in translating what they have learned in a group to actual situations they will encounter in daily life? How can you help members review what they have learned through a experience?

The Post-Group Stage

7. In your view, what responsibility does the group leader have in developing follow-up procedures and an evaluation program for a group? What are your thoughts on specific procedures you'd like to develop to evaluate the outcomes of a group?

8. What are some concrete advantages of arranging for a follow-up program as a part of a group experience?

9. List the key tasks of the group leader during the post-group period.

10. As a group counselor, what are your ideas on how you can combine evaluation approaches with improving yourself as a group practitioner? Discuss.

Some Guidelines on Learning the Differences
Between an Effective and an Ineffective Group

In the training of group counselors, I stress to them the role of leaders in teaching the group members how to assess continually the level of effectiveness of their group. Although there are not rigid characteristics of the "ideal group," it seems to me that there are certain characteristics that are a part of a working, productive, and effective group. The following are some questions and statements that you might pose to your students, so that they might begin asking the members of their groups to take a close look at how effective they are as members of the group. Leaders can challenge the members to continually evaluate their role in their group as well as determine the degree to which their group is productive.

1. There is a trust among members and with the leader, or at least if trust is absent, members are willing to express this. Do you trust most of the people in your group? How much trust do you feel toward your leader? How do you deal with the situation if you don't feel trust?

2. Goals are clear and determined by both the members and the leader. Is this true of your group? If not, what are you willing to do about this? If your own goals are fuzzy and general, what can you do to become more concrete and clarify what you want from your group?

3. Communication among members is open and direct. It involves an accurate expression of what is being experienced. Do you generally say what you think and feel? Do you hold back in fear of expressing yourself? How concrete and personal is the quality of your communication?

4. There is a feeling of inclusion, and excluded members are invited to become more participating members. Do many members in your group

feel excluded? Are there cliques that lead to the fragmentation of your group? How is this dealt with in group?

5. Leadership is a shared function in that participants feel free to initiate and to contribute to what occurs in their group. Do you lean on the leader for all direction? Are there power conflicts among the members or between members and the leader?

6. There is a willingness to disclose and share personal and meaningful material; people let themselves be known to others. Is your disclosure appropriate and honest, or is it forced? Do you keep yourself unknown? What kind of risks are you actually taking in the area of revealing yourself to others?

7. There is a feeling of togetherness in group; there is a close emotional bond that unites members. Cohesion is high as evidenced by a working together toward common ends, and an identification among the members. Do you feel a lack of caring and empathy? Do you feel distant and unconnected with others? If so, what do you do about this? What are you willing to do about it?

8. Conflict in the group, either among members or between the leader and members, is openly recognized and worked through. Are conflicts in your group smoothed over, with an open acknowledgment that there are sharp areas of disagreement? How do you attempt to resolve conflicts?

9. Members take on the responsibility for deciding on what action they will take to resolve their problems. Do you accept this responsibility or do you blame others for your personal difficulties and resist taking action that could lead to change?

10. Feedback is given freely and accepted without defensiveness. Do you give honest and direct feedback? How do you respond to the feedback you get from others? Is feedback given with care and sensitivity?

11. Confrontation occurs in such a way that those who confront share their own reactions to the people they confront. Confrontation is seen as a challenge to seriously examine one's behavior, not as an uncaring attack. How do you confront others? If you are confronted, how do you respond to it?

12. Members feel a sense of hope; they feel they can change. Do you experience this sense of faith and hope?

13. Group norms are cooperatively developed by the leader and the members; they are clear and designed to help members achieve their goals. Are you aware of the norms that function in your group? Do you have a chance to discuss the relevance of the group norms?

14. Participants use out-of-group time to work on problems raised in the group. To what degree are you applying what you learn in group to your

everyday life? Are you willing to do work and to practice outside of your group?

15. Participants say inside of group what they think and feel, and they avoid keeping secrets from the group *about* the group. Do you say to others outside of sessions things you are afraid or unwilling to say about the group at your sessions?

Unit Test on the Basic Elements of Group Process: An Overview

The following test items are taken from Part I, Chapters 1 through 5.

Types of Groups
1. A major difference between group therapy and group counseling lies in:
    a. the techniques employed to facilitate the process of interaction.
    * b. the goals of the process.
    c. the age of the participants.
    d. the theoretical orientation of the group leader.

2. Which type of group focuses on remediation, treatment, and personality reconstruction?
    a. support groups
    b. counseling groups
    * c. therapy groups
    d. self-help groups
    e. structured groups

3. Which of the following is an assumption of the self-help group?
    a. The medical model is an appropriate design to structure a group.
    b. A trained professional is essential to give the group direction.
    c. The group is viewed from a social microcosm theory.
    * d. Emphasis is upon a common identity based on a common life situation.
    e. Members should also be involved in individual therapy at the same time as they participate in a self-help group.

Ethical Issues in Group Work
4. What does a member have a right to expect before making the decision of whether or not to join a particular group?
    a. a discussion of the rights and responsibilities of group members
    b. a clear statement regarding the purpose of the group
    c. a pregroup interview
    d. information about the training and qualifications of the group leader
    * e. all of the above

5. An ethical practice for leaders to follow is to inform members that:
    a. once they join a group, they are required to remain in it until the group ends.
    b. they may terminate a group only when the leader gives consent to the member.

c. they are expected to exit from the group when the members take a vote.
* d. they should exit from the group only after they have discussed the matter in the group.

6. Confidentiality in groups is:
   a. a legal right of every member.
   b. something that members can be guaranteed.
* c. limited by state laws.
   d. an absolute that can never be broken for any reason.

7. Group leaders are expected to protect confidentiality of members by:
   a. clearly defining what confidentiality means.
   b. explaining to members why it is important.
   c. discussing the difficulties involved in enforcement.
* d. all of the above.

8. The ACA Code of Ethics specifically states which of the following to be unethical?
   a. socializing among group members
   b. leaderless groups
   c. using structured exercises in a group session
   d. using nonverbal exercises
* e. none of the above

9. What kind of clinical practice is endorsed by ASGW as a means of gaining supervised experience in group work?
   a. critiquing group tapes
   b. co-leading groups with supervision
   c. participating as a member in a group
   d. observing group counseling sessions
* e. all of the above

Overview of Group Leadership Skills

The following questions refer to the definition/description of specific group leadership skills. Match the definition with the most appropriate skill listed.

10. Opening up clear and direct communication among members; helping members to assume increasing responsibility for the group's direction
    a. suggesting
* b. facilitating
    c. goal setting
    d. giving feedback
    e. none of the above

11. Appraising the ongoing group process and the individual and group dynamics
    a. blocking
    b. facilitating
* c. evaluating

d. interpreting
   e. clarifying

12. Offering possible explanations for certain thoughts, feelings, and patterns of behavior
   * a. interpreting
   b. evaluating
   c. giving feedback
   d. active listening
   e. all of the above

13. Saying in slightly different words what a member has said to clarify its meaning
   a. reflecting feelings
   b. supporting
   c. facilitating
   * d. restating
   e. none of the above

14. Expressing concrete and honest reactions based on observation of members' behaviors
   a. disclosing oneself
   * b. giving feedback
   c. confronting
   d. clarifying
   e. summarizing

15. Grasping the essence of a message at both the feeling and the thinking levels; simplifying client statements by focusing on the core of the message
   a. active listening
   * b. clarifying
   c. restating
   d. summarizing
   e. interpreting

The next ten questions refer to the aims and desired outcomes of specific group leadership skills. Match the initial statement (desired outcomes) with the term that is the appropriate leadership skill.

16. To prepare members to assimilate, integrate, and apply in-group learning to everyday life
   a. modeling
   b. suggesting
   c. interpreting
   d. initiating
   * e. terminating

17. To help members sort out conflicting and confused feelings and thoughts; to arrive at a meaningful understanding of what is being communicated
   * a. clarifying
   b. interpreting
   c. evaluating
   d. suggesting
   e. none of the above

18. To foster trust in the therapeutic relationship; to communicate understanding and to encourage deeper levels of self-exploration
   a. questioning
   * b. empathizing
   c. reflecting feelings
   d. giving feedback
   e. summarizing

19. To let members know that they are heard and understood beyond the level of words
   a. active listening
   b. restating
   c. clarifying
   * d. reflecting feelings
   e. empathizing

20. To help members develop alternative courses of thinking and action
   a. giving feedback
   * b. suggesting
   c. interpreting
   d. supporting
   e. terminating

21. To offer an external view of how the person appears to others; to increase the client's self-awareness
   * a. giving feedback
   b. suggesting
   c. facilitating
   d. goal setting
   e. empathizing

22. To warn members of possible risks in group participation; to reduce these risks
   a. blocking
   b. evaluating
   * c. protecting
   d. facilitating
   e. none of the above

23. To avoid fragmentation and give direction to a session; to provide for continuity and meaning
    a. reflecting feelings
    * b. summarizing
    c. initiating
    d. blocking
    e. suggesting

24. To prevent needless group floundering; to increase the pace of group process
    a. modeling
    b. protecting
    c. blocking
    * d. initiating
    e. interpreting

25. To encourage deeper self-exploration; to provide a new perspective for considering and understanding one's behavior
    a. clarifying
    * b. interpreting
    c. confronting
    d. supporting
    e. suggesting

The Stages in the Development of a Group

26. Which stage is most closely associated with dealing with personal issues and translating insight into action both in the group and outside of it?
    a. transition
    b. consolidation
    c. orientation
    * d. working

27. Which stage has the focus of applying what has been learned in the group and putting it to use in everyday life?
    a. transition
    * b. consolidation
    c. orientation
    d. working

28. A group that is composed of people who are similar in age, type of problem, and personality characteristics can be called:
    * a. a homogeneous group.
    b. a heterogeneous group.
    c. an endogenous group.
    d. an androgynous group.

29. If the goal of a group is the simulation of everyday life, then it is a good idea to have:
    a. a homogeneous group.

* b. a heterogeneous group.
  c. an endogenous group.
  d. an androgynous group.

30. The basic criterion for the selection of group members is:
    * a. whether they will contribute to the group or whether they will be counterproductive.
    b. whether they are dependent or independent personalities.
    c. the absence of any neurotic symptoms.
    d. the degree to which the group leader likes the person.
    e. the degree to which the prospective member likes the leader.

31. Most writers agree that the foundation of the group is:
    a. the leader's skill in teaching members about group process.
    b. the motivation of members to work hard.
    c. the degree of enthusiasm of the group leader.
    * d. trust.
    e. group cohesion.

32. Regarding the factor of group cohesion, it can be said that:
    a. it can both help and hinder group process.
    b. when cohesiveness is not accompanied by a challenge to move forward, the group can reach a plateau.
    c. cohesion fosters other action-oriented behaviors such as risk taking, self-disclosure, confrontation, and translation of insight into action.
    * d. all of the above.

33. Interpreting the meaning of behavior patterns at appropriate times so that members will be able to engage in a deeper level of self-exploration and consider alternative behaviors is most critical at:
    a. the initial stage of a group.
    b. the transition stage.
    * c. the working stage.
    d. the consolidation stage.

34. When characteristics exist such as a high degree of cohesion, open communication, shared leadership functions, willingness to risk threatening material, and freely giving feedback and considering it nondefensively, it can be said that the group is at the:
    a. initial stage.
    b. transition stage.
    * c. working stage.
    d. final stage.

35. Which of the following is (are) considered therapeutic factor(s) of a group?
    a. hope
    b. commitment to change
    c. cognitive restructuring

d. self-disclosure
* e. all of the above

CHAPTER 6   THE PSYCHOANALYTIC APPROACH TO GROUPS

Lecture Notes and Outline for the Chapter
I. *Learning Objectives.* At the conclusion of reading and studying this chapter, the students are expected to have learned the essentials of the psychoanalytic approach to group work. This fundamental comprehension includes an understanding of the following:

   A. The key concepts of the psychoanalytic approach as they are related to group process;

   B. The role played by one's past in current development;

   C. A description of the nature of the unconscious and the role of unconscious factors in group process; a grasp of the basic procedures used by analytically oriented group practitioners to tap unconscious processes;

   D. The nature of anxiety and ways that it might manifest itself in the behavior of members;

   E. The role of dreams in group work;

   F. The nature of resistance and how to deal with it in groups;

   G. The process of both transference and countertransference as they are manifested in a group;

   H. The stages of the development of an analytic group;

   I. The specific roles and functions of the analytic group;

   J. Developmental stages as viewed by Freud and Erikson, and their implications for group work;

   K. The eight stages of development from birth to death with a knowledge of the implications of the psychosexual and psychosocial stages for working with individuals in a group;

   L. The contemporary trends in psychoanalytic group theory, with a focus on object-relations theory and with special consideration given to implications for group work with both borderline personality and narcissistic personality disorders;

   M. The major contributions and limitations of psychoanalytic group therapy in working with culturally diverse populations; and

   N. The importance of adapting psychoanalytic techniques to working with culturally diverse clients.

II. *Key Terms in This Chapter.* Students can be expected to clearly identify, define, describe, and explain the following terms within the context of the psychoanalytic approach as this model is applied to groups:
- the unconscious
- anxiety
- free association
- interpretation
- dream analysis
- manifest content of dreams
- latent content of dreams
- resistance
- group analysis
- transference
- countertransference
- insight
- working through
- catharsis
- alternate session
- free association
- self psychology
- borderline disorders
- ego-defense mechanism

- psychosexual development
- psychosocial development
- developmental model
- developmental task
- life crisis
- oral stage
- basic sense of trust
- anal stage
- autonomy
- phallic stage
- latency stage
- genital stage
- personal identity
- identity diffusion
- ego integrity
- ego psychology
- object relations theory
- narcissistic disorders

III. *Lecture Outline: Notes and Comments*
   A. Introduction
      1. Before our discussion of each theory chapter, I typically ask students to respond to a few items to which they had the strongest reaction on the pre-chapter primer and self-inventory found in the *Student Manual*. This is a handy way to get some view of the degree to which students agree or disagree with the major concepts of each theory. It can be used as catalyst material for group discussion.
      2. Often we will discuss some items on the pre-chapter primer at the beginning of the lecture/discussion and then again after they have had more exposure to the model, especially after they have had some experiential practice with the therapeutic approach in a group situation.
      3. Another device I use to introduce students to the theory in a general way is to have them read over the charts in the *Student Manual* on the initial, working, and final stages of a group. This chart serves as a useful review device after the students have studied the chapter.
      4. Also in the *Student Manual* is a section that summarizes the basic assumptions of the approach. I find this to be a convenient way to review the highlights and key concepts of each theory, and it also introduces the students to the underlying assumptions of each therapeutic approach.

B. Influence of the Past
   1. In my own lectures I share with students the value that I place on knowing and understanding how past factors are critical in understanding the person's current struggles.
   2. I also stress the pitfalls in getting lost in and dwelling on the past, especially if it is done in a way to avoid accepting responsibility for one's behavior.
   3. My lectures are brief, and broken up with an opportunity to practice the concept. For example, in the *Student Manual* I describe a technique that I often use in groups—writing the outline and preface to the "Book of Your Life." This focuses the students on their own past, on the significant events that have influenced them, and on ways that their past may still be alive today.

C. The Unconscious
   1. Although group counseling tends to deal with conscious factors (and not unconscious dynamics), I think it is essential for students to understand that dealing with conscious factors exclusively is not the entire story.
   2. Lectures might include some evidence for the existence of the unconscious, arguments for and against the role of the unconscious as a factor in group work, and the values inherent in a here-and-now versus a there-and-then approach and vice versa.

D. Anxiety
   1. In what specific ways is anxiety revealed in the context of a group? What is the analytic view of anxiety?
   2. What are examples of specific situations in a group that might be anxiety-producing?

E. Ego-defense Mechanisms
   1. Students can identify the most common ego defenses that they see manifested in groups. A useful discussion is to look at the purposes that these defenses serve.
   2. Discuss ego defenses in terms of the adaptive value they serve.

F. Resistance
   1. In class discussions, I tend to focus on how resistance manifests itself in various ways through group members' behaviors. I like to spend time talking about the function that resistance serves and I encourage students to acquire an attitude of respect toward member resistance.
   2. Students can be asked to identify their own sources of resistance and to explore this in small groups. I put emphasis on therapeutic strategies in dealing with resistance in groups.

G. Transference
   1. Discuss how transference is seen as a central issue in the analytic group. Have the students had experiences in this realm

in their experience as group members? How have they dealt with their own transference either in a group situation or in situations outside of a group?
   2. In class discussions, we explore the therapeutic value of identifying transference relationships as they become evident within a group structure. The discussion focuses on creative ways of dealing with member transference in a group setting.
H. Countertransference
   1. I typically focus on the role of countertransference and alert the students to common types and manifestations of this phenomenon. Students can select the kind of client they'd expect to encounter the greatest deal of difficulty with, become this client in a role-playing situation, and have others attempt to deal with this "problem client."
   2. I bring out for discussion the common signs of countertransference in leader's behavior. The purpose of this discussion is to invite students to look at their own potential issues that are likely to interfere with objectively working with certain group members.
   3. It is useful to point out the relationship between becoming aware of countertransference reactions and insight. Insight and working through are other concepts that we examine. We typically discuss the role of insight in change of behavior or personality. I ask students to think about and share insights they've had and what they have done with them. Give examples of acting on insights. Also, give examples of having insights alone without translating them into behavior change.
I. Free Association
   1. In addition to discussing the concept and technique of free association, I attempt to have students experience this process, largely through sentence completion work.
J. Interpretation
   1. Consider mentioning the dangers of interpretations that are inaccurate, poorly timed, or "forced on members" by dogmatic leaders.
   2. I also stress the values and the potential problems of the group members' sharing interpretations for others in the group.
K. Dream Analysis
   1. In lecture you may want to compare and contrast the Freudian approach to working with dreams in a group with the Gestalt approach.
   2. Some students have kept a dream journal and looked for themes in their dreams. This can provide a framework for some experiential work in small groups in class.

3. The *Student Manual* provides some specific ways of working with dreams in a group.

L. Role and Functions of the Group Leader
1. We focus on the primary role of the analytic therapist in facilitating the process of uncovering unconscious dynamics of the members' present behavior.
2. There is usually some lively discussion on the advantages and disadvantages of the analytic group therapist's stance that is characterized by objectivity, warm detachment, and relative anonymity.

M. Developmental Stages and Their Implications for Group Work
1. I have found it useful to combine the Freudian view of life stages with those described by Erikson. Freud describes the *psychosexual* stages, which have particular relevance during the first five years of life. Erikson seems to take off where Freud stopped with his *psychosocial* stages, which extend to death. In my own lectures I merely highlight the key crises of each stage and at the same time alert the students to look for these developmental crises in individuals in the group.
2. It is useful to ask students to apply the critical tasks of the various stages of life to their own development. Catalyst questions for small group interaction include: What are some of the major turning points in your life? How do you see events in your past as influencing you today? What are some personal developmental struggles you have had that you think will affect your work with members of your groups? Do you think that you can help clients to explore their developmental concerns if you have not experienced similar problems?

N. Contemporary Trends in Psychoanalytic Group Theory
1. Although object-relations theory can be complex and difficult for many students (and instructors) to grasp, it is a good idea to at least introduce students to the idea that psychoanalytic theory continues to develop. An interesting focus of discussion is on the role of the quality of the interactions between the child and the mother in the first three years of life. Mahler's perspective on early development, especially her views on the process of separation and individuation, are useful in exploring the influence of these early experiences on later relationships.
2. Perhaps a discussion of borderline and narcissistic individuals is the most important aspect of the contemporary trends in analytic thinking. I tend to focus on the implications for group work with borderline and narcissistic members. What are the potential problems of including such personalities in a group? How can group therapy be particularly helpful for borderline and narcissistic individuals?

O. Evaluation of the Psychoanalytic Model
1. With each approach, my aim is to get students to appreciate both the limitations and contributions of that approach to group counseling. In dealing with psychoanalytic group work, I ask students to discuss the major concepts that they find helpful in facilitating groups.
2. As a part of this evaluation, I ask students to think about the contributions and limitations of the approach in working with culturally diverse group members. Good catalyst questions are: How can psychoanalytically oriented group therapy, if modified, be appropriate for culturally diverse populations? What are some potential difficulties in applying a psychoanalytic approach with minority clients?

Focus Questions for Chapter 6: The Psychoanalytic Approach to Groups
1. Show historically how the psychoanalytic approach has important connections to all of the other theories that will be discussed in this textbook. In what way can an understanding of psychoanalytic concepts help group leaders make sense of what occurs in a group setting?
2. Mention and briefly discuss some advantages of a group format over an individual analysis that utilizes psychoanalytic concepts and techniques.
3. Summarize the psychoanalytic position with respect to the role and influence of the past as a key factor of present development. How is the past dealt with in the analytic group?
4. What is the basic goal of the analytic group?
5. Describe how free association is used to uncover repressed and unconscious material in an analytic group.
6. In what way is interpretation a basic procedure in psychoanalytically oriented groups?
7. What is the rationale underlying analytic dream work? How are dreams typically dealt with in the analytic group?
8. Give some typical ways that resistance is manifested in the analytic group. What are some forms that resistance takes? How do group analysts deal with resistance?
9. Discuss the group as an ideal way to recognize and deal with *multiple transferences*. How does the analytic group become a repetition of significant events from the original family? What is the analytic perspective on interpreting and working through transferences?
10. What are the primary roles and functions of the leader of an analytic group? From your vantage point, how comfortable would you be in assuming these functions?

11. How can an understanding of the Freudian and psychosocial views of development be beneficial to the group leader as he seeks to conceptualize the dynamics occurring within his group?

12. Pick one of Erikson's stages of development and discuss what issues a group member might have that would correspond to that stage. How would you help that individual to deal with his struggles in a constructive way?

13. Write a critical evaluation of the psychoanalytic model of group. Include factors such as the unique aspects of the approach, the contributions and the limitations of the model, and basic problems in using the model.

14. List and discuss a few concepts and procedures that you would most want to include in your leadership style based on the analytic approach.

Quiz: Comprehension Check
In the space provided, place a *T* if the statement is true and an *F* if the statement is false, within the *psychoanalytic perspective*.

(T) 1. A key method in analytic group work for unlocking unconscious material is free association.

(T) 2. Working with the past is considered to be essential in the psychoanalytic group.

(F) 3. The analytic group leader tends to be open about his or her private life, for this type of self-disclosure is seen as facilitating transference relationships.

(F) 4. Erikson's stage of "autonomy versus shame and doubt" corresponds to Freud's phallic stage.

(T) 5. The majority of an adolescent's struggles can be seen as relating to the development of a personal identity.

(F) 6. A person in Erikson's sixth stage of development (young adulthood) is typically undergoing an identity crisis.

(F) 7. Freud's anal stage is basically the same as the period Erikson characterizes as one of trust versus mistrust.

(F) 8. The key crisis of the adolescent period is integrity versus disgust.

(T) 9. Freud provided a model to understand the developmental processes during the early childhood years.

(F) 10. Erikson tends to agree with Freud's emphasis on sexual stages as opposed to social stages.

Quiz: The Psychoanalytic Approach to Groups

NOTE: Some of the multiple-choice items also appear in each of the chapter's comprehension checks in the *Student Manual*.

1. The goal of the analytic group is to work toward:
   a. adequate social adjustment.
   b. a structuring of one's personality.
   c. uncovering early experiences.

d. achieving intense feelings in the here and now.
* e. both (b) and (c).

2. The key to understanding personality problems is:
   a. through the use of diagnostic testing.
   b. by asking members to report what they are feeling.
 * c. the unconscious.
   d. by analysis of resistance.
   e. the empathy of the group leader.

3. In a group setting, free association could be used for:
   a. uncovering repressed material.
   b. encouraging spontaneity among the members.
   c. working on dreams in the group.
   d. interacting with one another in the group.
 * e. all of the above.

4. Interpretations in the analytic group are made by:
   a. the group leader.
   b. the member who is working on a problem.
   c. by all of the members at times.
 * d. all of the above.

5. Interpretations are made of:
   a. dreams.
   b. resistances that become evident in a group.
   c. reactions members have toward one another.
   d. reactions toward the group leader.
 * e. all of the above.

6. Psychoanalytic dream work consists of:
   a. asking the member to act out all parts of his dream.
 * b. interpretation of the latent meaning of the dream.
   c. having the member analyze and interpret his own dream.
   d. the leader avoiding giving any interpretations of the dream.
   e. both (c) and (d).

7. The first person credited with applying psychoanalytic principles and techniques to groups is:
   a. Sigmund Freud.
 * b. Alexander Wolf.
   c. W. R. Bion.
   d. Erik Erikson.
   e. S. H. Foulkes.

8. Resistance in the psychoanalytic approach is viewed as:
   a. an unconscious dynamic.
   b. a conscious refusal of a member to explore a topic that is threatening.
   c. a basic part of the analytic process.

d. the group's refusal to cooperate with the leader.
 * e. both (a) and (c).

9. Transference in the analytic group is viewed as:
   a. a sign that therapy is ineffective.
   b. the core of group work.
   c. a means to uncover past conflicts.
 * d. both (b) and (c).

10. The teaching technique whereby the group leader suggests the meaning of certain behaviors is known as:
    a. transference.
    b. countertransference.
    c. rationalization.
    d. free association.
 * e. none of the above.

11. An advantage of a group is that:
    a. multiple transference can be formed.
    b. the group becomes a family of yesterday.
    c. members can benefit from one another's work.
    d. members can learn to identify their own transferences.
 * e. all of the above.

12. In the analytic group, countertransference is seen as:
    a. a sign that the members have unfinished business with the group leader.
    b. a sign that the group leader is not competent to lead the group.
    c. evidence that members are reminded of key figures in their early years in the form of the leader.
    d. all of the above.
 * e. none of the above.

13. Insight and the process of working through are considered:
    a. unessential in group work.
 * b. necessary before members can be considered ready to leave the group.
    c. necessary for the therapist, but not for the members.
    d. to be things that are accomplished only after a person leaves the group.
    e. both (c) and (d).

14. W. R. Bion's method of interpretation of group process consisted of:
    a. dealing with the dynamics of the individual.
    b. dealing with ways in which an individual reacted in the group in similar ways to how he or she acted in the family situation.
 * c. dealing with the group as a whole rather than individual member's reactions.
    d. dealing with traumatic situations in early childhood.

15. Bion observed three basic assumptions that groups develop on their way to becoming a "work group," including:
    a. autonomy, inclusion-exclusion, struggle for control.
    * b. dependency, fight-flight, pairing.
    c. trust versus mistrust, bonding, working through.
    d. milling around, identity, cohesion.
    e. dependency, struggle for identity, autonomy.

16. Many analytically oriented group therapists have a leadership style that is characterized by:
    * a. objectivity, warm detachment, and relative anonymity.
    b. objectivity, aloofness, and strict anonymity.
    c. subjectivity, mutuality, and self-disclosure.
    d. rationality, impersonality, and coolness.

17. Which is *not* a part of the stages of analytic groups?
    a. creating rapport through sharing of dreams
    b. interaction through interpersonal free association
    * c. analysis of ego states
    d. analysis of resistance
    e. analysis of transference

18. When members meet for a session without the formal leader, this is known in analytic circles as:
    a. the member-oriented session.
    * b. the alternate session.
    c. organized resistance.
    d. self-motivated interaction session.
    e. none of the above.

19. Which function is generally *not* carried out by an analytic group leader?
    a. pointing out evidence of resistance
    b. relinquishing leadership by encouraging members to interact with one another
    c. making interpretations
    * d. demanding contracts from each member as a prerequisite to joining the group
    e. asking questions

20. Which statement(s) is (are) *untrue* of the analytic group?
    * a. It is generally a homogeneous group.
    b. It is a long-term group.
    c. It is focused on uncovering unconscious dynamics.
    d. It encourages the development of transferences.

21. The psychoanalytic group can be applied to:
    a. a neurotic population.
    b. people who are relatively well-functioning.
    c. adolescents.
    * d. all of the above.

22. Which of the following is *not* one of Erikson's eight stages of development?
    a. trust versus mistrust
    b. generativity versus stagnation
  * c. integrity versus role diffusion
    d. intimacy versus isolation

23. The major task for a child of preschool age is:
    a. to engage in social tasks.
    b. to explore the world.
    c. to achieve a sense of industry.
  * d. to establish a sense of competence.

24. The "identity crisis" is a hallmark of:
  * a. adolescence.
    b. young adulthood.
    c. school age children.
    d. all of the above.

25. A person who is Erikson's "middle age" stage:
  * a. is dealing with accepting the inevitability of his own death.
    b. often suffers from a feeling of hopelessness.
    c. is adjusting to retirement.
    d. is concerned with achieving intimacy in his relationships.

CHAPTER 7   ADLERIAN GROUP COUNSELING

Lecture Notes and Outline for the Chapter

I. *Learning Objectives.* The basic objective of this chapter is for the students to have an introductory knowledge of the concepts and procedures involved in the Adlerian approach to group work. Some specific objectives include:

   A. To understand the Adlerian view of the person and the implications of this perspective for the practice of group counseling;

   B. To be able to identify the basic assumptions and key concepts of the Adlerian approach to groups;

   C. To be able to identify the common denominators of the Adlerian approach with the other therapeutic approaches and models;

   D. To describe the rationale for group counseling from the Adlerian perspective; to describe the phases of the Adlerian group;

   E. To describe the role of the Adlerian group counselor; and

   F. To have an understanding of how Adlerian concepts are applied to family counseling.

II. *Key Terms to Identify and Define*
- striving for superiority
- power and mastery
- holism
- creativity and choice
- phenomenology
- teleology
- social interest
- inferiority/superiority
- lifestyle
- family constellation
- community feeling
- early recollections
- basic mistakes
- lifestyle investigation
- goal alignment
- insight
- interpretation
- reorientation
- encouragement
- initial interview
- commitment
- the question

III. *Lecture Outline: Notes and Comments*
   A. Introduction
      1. As was stated in the last chapter, I typically begin by asking students to share their reactions to the prechapter self-inventories found in the *Student Manual*. The overview charts on the stages of group development for each theory, along with the summary or basic assumptions of each approach, are especially helpful for discovering areas of interest in the class.
   B. Key Concepts
      1. The key concepts that I stress are feelings of inferiority, compensation, developing a unique style of life, and striving for power and status.
      2. The lecture can be supplemented with experiential exercises in which students apply the central concepts of this approach to themselves.
      3. The concepts and techniques, along with the stages of the Adlerian group, are topics that can be highlighted.
      4. Students find it interesting to focus on early recollections, family constellation, place in their family, and influence of the family on their development. Since these are major contributions of this approach, students can benefit from experiential work in small groups with this as a focus.
   C. Application of Adlerian Principles to Group Work
      1. Since the Adlerian approach is basically a social one, we discuss ways that group counseling fits the spirit of the Adlerian model. Stress is given to factors in a group setting such as:
         - developing a sense of belonging,
         - working on problems that are interpersonal in nature,
         - using the group and other members to make and follow through with commitments to change behavior patterns.
      2. Adlerians often begin a group with a structured interview to obtain information about the family constellation, early recollections, life goals, and childhood experiences. To make this real for the students, I ask them to review the lifestyle

assessment given in the *Student Manual* and then have them form small groups to discuss salient points in their own developmental history. This is an excellent way for students to get to know one another, and it is a way to generate material for group work. As much as is possible, I attempt to get the students experientially involved with the material. We have found that the cognitive processing and discussions take on more reality and meaning when the students become personally involved with the concepts they are studying.

Focus Questions for Chapter 7: Adlerian Group Counseling

1. Explain Adler's holistic view of the person in terms of its implications for group and family therapy.

2. "Adler believed that *what* we are born with is not crucial, but rather the *use* we make of our natural endowment." Explain this statement and give your own views on an individual's capacity for creativity and choice.

3. What is meant by a "phenomenological orientation" toward therapy? How would a group leader with this orientation relate to his group members?

4. Explain Adler's concept of "social interest." How can a group be an ideal place for the development of an individual's capacity for social interest?

5. List and then discuss and critically evaluate some of the *basic assumptions* underlying the Adlerian approach to groups.

6. Discuss some of the *basic differences* between the Adlerian and psychoanalytic approaches to group therapy.

7. Discuss the role of *power* as a key factor in Adlerian theory. How is this dealt with in groups?

8. What is the meaning of the lifestyle? Explain how one's lifestyle is based on one's inferiority feeling and the "striving for superiority." How is this unique lifestyle explored in an Adlerian group?

9. Describe the major goals of Adlerian group counseling.

10. List and discuss the *four phases* that are typical in the stages of development of the Adlerian group.

11. Describe the concept of *"goal alignment."*

12. Describe how the exploration of the *family constellation* and the *earliest recollections* are a basic part of the analysis and assessment of individuals in the Adlerian group.

13. How is *insight* viewed by the Adlerians?

14. How is interpretation done in the Adlerian group? How is the style of interpretation different from the classical Freudian analysis?
15. How is the *encouragement process* a basic part of the Adlerian group?
16. Discuss the *role* of the Adlerian group counselor. How does this role fit for *you* as a group leader?
17. Write a critical evaluation of the Adlerian model. Include in this critique both its contributions and limitations, and aspects of this approach that you'd most want to incorporate into your own group leading.

Quiz: Comprehension Check
In the space provided, place a *T* if the statement is true and *F* if the statement is false.

(T) 1. In Adlerian counseling, there tends to be a greater emphasis placed on interpersonal factors than on intrapersonal dynamics.
(F) 2. The Adlerian counselor assumes an objective stance in seeking to understand his group members.
(T) 3. The term "social interest" refers to the attitudes an individual holds with regard to dealing with the social world.
(F) 4. A major emphasis of *current* Adlerian therapy is compensating for feelings of inferiority.
(F) 5. The goal of Adlerian family counseling is to help each family member to become a self-actualized individual.
(T) 6. Adler was a politically and socially oriented psychiatrist who showed a great deal of concern for the common person.
(T) 7. The socio-teleological approach implies that people are primarily social beings motivated by social forces.
(F) 8. The Adlerian approach contends that we can be understood best by looking at critical turning points during the first five years of life.
(T) 9. Another phrase for the Adlerian approach is "individual psychology."
(F) 10. Teleology is a concept that refers to deterministic explanations of current behavior.

Quiz: The Adlerian Approach to Groups
1. Adler developed his approach from:
   * a. the psychoanalytic approach.
     b. the behavioral approach.
     c. the rational-oriented therapies.
     d. all of the above.

2. The Adlerian approach stresses:
   a. unconscious factors.
   b. power and status.
   c. social determinants of personality.

d. irrational impulses.
* e. both (b) and (c).

3. Adler stressed:
   a. the value of transference for group therapy.
* b. the purposeful nature of behavior.
   c. the role of biological determinants of behavior.
   d. two of the above.
   e. none of the above.

4. According to Adler, feelings of inferiority:
   a. are the wellsprings of creativity.
   b. lead to the development of a unique lifestyle.
   c. lead to some form of comprehension.
   d. are related to power.
* e. all of the above.

5. Who developed Adlerian group methods?
   a. Viktor Frankl
* b. Rudolf Dreikurs
   c. Abraham Maslow
   d. J. L. Moreno
   e. none of the above

6. Which of the following is *not* a basic characteristic of the Adlerian approach to group work?
   a. establishing a therapeutic relationship
   b. analysis of individual dynamics
   c. insight
* d. developing group rapport through sharing of dreams
   e. a reorientation

7. Goal alignment refers to the state whereby:
   a. all the members develop common goals.
* b. both the leader's and the member's goals are the same.
   c. members actually carry out new behavior beyond the group session.
   d. members accept the goals of society by adjusting to the dominant norms.

8. In Adlerian group work, analysis and assessment:
   a. are ways of exploring an individual's dynamics.
   b. are ongoing processes.
   c. are considered as detrimental to group process.
   d. are seen as neither necessary nor desirable.
* e. both (a) and (b).

9. The idea that individuals are to be viewed as a unity, or an indivisible whole is known as:
   a. ego integrity.
* b. holism.

    c. self-actualization.
    d. phenomenology.

10. All of the following are goals of Adlerian group therapy except:
    a. to increase self-esteem.
    b. to develop social interest.
    c. to establish and maintain an empathic relationship between group leader and member.
  * d. to help group members become self-actualized.

11. Another phrase for Adlerian psychology is:
    a. social psychology.
  * b. individual psychology.
    c. phenomenological psychology.
    d. social-behavioral psychology.

12. Which of the following is *not* a key concept of the Adlerian approach?
    a. holism
    b. creativity and choice
  * c. psychic determinism
    d. teleology
    e. social interest

13. Which concept helps us to explain how all human behavior fits together so that there is some consistency to actions?
  * a. lifestyle
    b. ego
    c. social interest
    d. holism

14. What best describes the Adlerian view of the therapeutic relationship?
    a. The therapist is considered the expert.
    b. The therapist should always maintain objectivity as a way of fostering transference.
    c. The therapist is seen as a behavioral engineer.
  * d. The therapeutic relationship is one between equals.

15. The individual analysis consists of:
    a. exploration of the family constellation.
    b. asking clients to report their earliest recollections.
    c. uncovering basic mistakes.
    d. exploration of one's lifestyle.
  * e. all of the above.

16. In Adlerian counseling, the group leader's main task during the assessment phases is:
  * a. to integrate data from the lifestyle investigation.
    b. to interpret the latent meanings of dreams.
    c. to administer projective tests.
    d. to develop specific behavioral goals and a treatment plan.
    e. both (c) and (d).

17. The Adlerian view of insight is that:
    a. personality is not changed unless there is insight.
    b. insight is a necessary prerequisite for behavioral change.
    * c. insight is understanding translated into constructive action.
    d. insight always follows a release of intense feelings.
    e. insight is primarily an intellectual awareness of causes of personality problems.

18. In the Adlerian group, interpretation is:
    a. a technique that facilitates the process of gaining insight.
    b. focused on the here-and-now behavior.
    c. done in relationship to the lifestyle.
    d. related to one's family and early recollections.
    * e. all of the above.

19. In the Adlerian group, the reorientation phase consists of:
    a. considering alternative attitudes, beliefs, and goals.
    b. reeducating members in becoming more effective in dealing with the tasks of life.
    c. encouraging clients to take action.
    d. challenging members to take risks.
    * e. all of the above.

20. The primary role of the Adlerian group leader is:
    a. interpreting resistances.
    b. uncovering repressed material.
    * c. to challenge the beliefs and goals of the members.
    d. to develop a treatment plan and evaluate results.
    e. both (a) and (b).

21. Which statement(s) is (are) *false* regarding the role of the Adlerian group leader?
    a. The leader is encouraged to keep somewhat anonymous.
    b. The leader adopts a passive role.
    c. The leader serves as a model.
    d. The leader uses active intervention methods.
    * e. Both (a) and (b).

22. Adlerian therapy has some similarities to which therapy(ies)?
    a. Gestalt therapy
    b. person-centered approach
    c. rational emotive behavior therapy
    d. humanistic approach
    * e. all of the above

23. Adlerian and behavior therapies have what in common?
    a. Both give attention to positive reinforcement.
    b. Both stress the modeling role of the group leader.
    c. Both involve assessment and analysis.

* d. All of the above.
  e. None of the above.

24. Adlerian and reality therapies have what in common?
    a. Both include an interest in early recollections.
    b. Both focus on commitment as a prerequisite for change.
    c. Both involve the use of encouragement.
    d. Both focus on working through transference.
* e. Both (b) and (c).

25. Adlerian therapy and the person-centered approach have what in common?
    a. Both include an interest in the unity of behavior.
    b. Both are based on a growth model.
    c. Both are subjective perspectives.
    d. Both stress the value of listening and empathy.
* e. All of the above.

CHAPTER 8   PSYCHODRAMA

Lecture Notes and Outline
I. *Learning Objectives.* After completing the chapter, students are expected to:
   A. Be familiar with the key concepts of psychodrama;
   B. Have a knowledge of the specific techniques typically used in role-playing situations and psychodrama;
   C. Be able to identify situations in which psychodrama would be an appropriate intervention;
   D. Identify the roles and functions of the psychodrama leader;
   E. Describe the steps involved in setting up a psychodrama, actually conducting one, and evaluating a psychodrama; and
   F. Identify those elements from this approach that are of value to the individual; and to critically evaluate the approach.

II. *Key Terms to Identify and Define*
   - catharsis
   - insight
   - reality testing
   - protagonist
   - auxiliary egos
   - encounter
   - tele
   - role theory
   - role training
   - role playing
   - spontaneity
   - audience
   - role reversal
   - doubling
   - mirror technique
   - magic shop technique
   - future projection technique
   - replay
   - surplus reality
   - creativity

III. *Lecture Outline: Notes and Comments*
   A. Introduction
      1. Begin with the basic assumptions underlying the method of psychodrama, which are summarized in the *Student Manual.*
      2. Typically, I ask students if they have had any contact with psychodrama, what they know about the approach, and what they'd like to know about it.
   B. Key Concepts in Group Process: Psychodrama
      1. Give a brief overview of how psychodrama works, discussing the focus on action, here and now, spontaneity, reliving experiences, catharsis, and feedback.
      2. I also mention briefly the role of the psychodrama leader, and the functions of other members in a psychodrama.
      3. I usually stress both the values and the limitations, as well as some cautions, in this lecture. I encourage students to *experience* as a member a psychodrama, before they attempt to introduce these powerful techniques in a group they are leading.
   C. Applications: Techniques and Process of the Phases of Psychodrama
      1. Generally, I find it best to give a description of the three phases involved in a psychodrama: (1) the warming-up process; (2) the action phase; and (3) the discussion period. After giving a picture of how psychodrama works in theory, I ask for volunteers for a demonstration of the method. The kind of work I prefer to do as a class demonstration generally involves focusing on relationships that students would like to understand better and improve. I take care to see that students who are involved are given opportunities for adequate closure.
      2. Some of the basic techniques that I demonstrate in class and then have students practice in smaller groups are: self-presentation, role reversal, soliloquy, rehearsing out loud, and future projection. I prefer to use techniques such as mirroring, doubling, alter egos, and multiple doubles in the context of an actual psychodrama. For this, I prefer a weekend workshop setting, where the format can become more intense than in a classroom setting.
      3. I also point out some basic similarities with psychodrama and other modalities, especially Gestalt therapy, TA, and other experiential approaches.
      4. Questions I typically ask students are: What are some concepts and techniques of psychodrama/role playing that appeal to you the most? What are the aspects that you'd like to incorporate into your style of leading?

Focus Questions for Chapter 8: Psychodrama
1. Discuss briefly the following key concepts in group process as they relate to *psychodrama*.
   a. encounter and action
   b. spontaneity and creativity
   c. dealing with the present
   d. catharsis and insight
   e. reality testing

2. List and briefly explain the basic assumptions underlying the psychodrama approach to group work.

3. What are some of the advantages of the action-oriented methods of psychodrama where members act out their conflicts and problems as opposed to merely talking about these occasions?

4. What are the basic functions and tasks of the psychodrama leader? Explain.

5. Define the term *protagonist*.

6. What are *auxiliary egos* and how are they used in psychodrama? Explain briefly the functions of auxiliary egos.

7. How can the group (or audience) also benefit from the work a given member does in a psychodrama? Discuss the role of the members in giving support and feedback to the protagonist.

8. Describe the essentials involved in these three phases of a psychodrama:
   a. the warm-up process
   b. the action phase
   c. the discussion phase

9. Why is a warm-up period necessary for an effective psychodrama? Describe a few warm-up procedures you might use if you were to design a psychodrama.

10. Define and briefly describe each of the following psychodrama procedures and techniques that are typically employed during the action phase:
    a. self-presentation
    b. role reversal
    c. soliloquy
    d. doubling
    e. mirror technique
    f. magic shop
    g. future projection
    h. replay
    i. role training

11. If you were using psychodrama, and if members completed a segment of work, what are some things you'd want those members to focus on? How would you take care to see that members were not left with unnecessary unresolved feelings? How would you include the rest of the participants in the discussion phase?

12. *When* do you think that psychodrama methods are called for? With what population do you see this method as being particularly appropriate? Are there some populations that you'd not want to employ psychodrama techniques with? Why or why not?

13. Write a personal evaluation of the psychodrama method. In your critique mention aspects you most value as well as aspects you least like. What are some of the unique contributions of this method? What are its basic limitations? What do you most want to draw from this model? How might you incorporate some of the concepts and techniques from psychodrama into your own personal style as a group leader? What are some applications of psychodrama in multicultural settings?

Quiz: Comprehension Check
Indicate whether each of the following statements is *T* (true) or *F* (false) as it applies to *psychodrama*.

(F) 1. Fritz Perls is the originator of psychodrama.
(T) 2. Psychodrama has a here-and-now focus.
(F) 3. The group leader, not the member, generally selects the particular problem or event a member will explore in a psychodrama.
(F) 4. Psychodrama is an inappropriate therapeutic technique for children.
(T) 5. Members of the audience or group typically act as alter-egos, provide support, give feedback, and share their own emotional experience to a psychodrama event with a protagonist.
(T) 6. In many ways, psychodrama was the precursor of many other group approaches.
(T) 7. Moreno's action-oriented methods represent an extension of the psychoanalytic approach in that his methods are grounded in psychoanalytic concepts.
(F) 8. It is the group leader, not the protagonist, who generally selects the group members who will serve as auxiliary egos.
(T) 9. Psychodrama can be useful as a method of instruction for mental health professionals.
(F) 10. Due to the nature of psychodrama, it is not appropriate to use its concepts or procedures in working with a family group.

Quiz: Psychodrama
1. Psychodrama was developed by:
    a. Fritz Perls.
    b. Carl Rogers.
*   c. J. L. Moreno.

    d. Sidney Jourard.
    e. none of the above.

2. Which statement(s) is (are) *false* as applied to psychodrama?
    a. The therapy is an action-oriented method.
    b. The therapy is characterized by a here-and-now focus.
    c. Emphasis is on catharsis and insight.
  * d. Emphasis is on identifying ego states.
    e. Two of the above.

3. Psychodrama began:
    a. at the Esalen Institute in Big Sur, California.
  * b. in Vienna.
    c. in the Soviet Union.
    d. in Germany.
    e. none of the above.

4. The psychodrama method emphasizes:
  * a. spontaneity and creativity.
    b. an intellectual understanding of the causes of conflicts.
    c. a way of challenging irrational beliefs.
    d. understanding life scripts.
    e. all of the above.

5. The emphasis on acting in psychodrama is for the purpose of:
    a. freeing an individual.
    b. providing members with a new understanding of their problems.
    c. providing a here-and-now focus.
    d. allowing full expression of feelings.
  * e. all of the above.

6. The past is dealt with:
    a. by dwelling on causal factors of current problems.
    b. by bringing it into the present.
    c. by talking about possible reasons for feelings.
    d. by reenacting the event and reexperiencing earlier feelings.
  * e. both (b) and (d).

7. How is catharsis a part of psychodrama?
    a. Pent-up feelings are released through acting.
    b. Catharsis is not seen as necessary or desirable.
    c. Catharsis is facilitated by the use of certain techniques designed to intensify feelings.
    d. Catharsis is useful only after members fully understand what is causing a particular problem.
  * e. both (a) and (c).

8. The role of the psychodrama group leader is:
    a. to be a producer.
    b. to be a catalyst/facilitator.
    c. to be an observer/analyzer.

* d. all of the above.
     e. none of the above.

9. Which is *not* generally a function of the psychodrama director?
   a. to warm up the group before action takes place
   b. to coach other members to act as doubles
   c. to offer suggestions regarding what scenes might be enacted
   * d. to attack the illogical beliefs of members
   e. to lead a sharing session after an action segment

10. The protagonist is:
    * a. the person selected to work.
    b. the symbolic figure in a member's life that antagonizes the member.
    c. the group member who serves as an alter-ego.
    d. the director when he or she is role-playing with the member who is working.
    e. the symbolic figure who is the target of anger.

11. The auxiliary ego is:
    * a. a group member who plays symbolic roles.
    b. an inner part of the member that is in conflict.
    c. the person who is chosen to work on a conflict.
    d. played at all times by the director.

12. The function(s) of the auxiliary ego is (are):
    a. to represent an absent person.
    b. to double for the protagonist.
    c. to help the protagonist intensify feelings.
    * d. all of the above.
    e. none of the above.

13. According to psychodrama:
    a. members of the group can profit only if they are directly involved in reenacting an event.
    * b. members of the group can benefit in vicarious ways by observing the work of others.
    c. members will change their behavior only if they develop a contract that specifies homework assignments.
    d. unless a problem is solved, the psychodrama is a failure.

14. A danger of psychodrama is (are):
    a. participants being left without adequate closure.
    b. misuse of power on the part of the leader.
    c. pushing people beyond the level to which they want to work.
    d. breaking down defenses without substituting constructive ways to deal with anxiety.
    * e. all of the above.

15. The purpose of role reversal is:
    a. to create empathy.
    b. to help the protagonist understand the role of a significant person.

       c. to make a therapeutic intervention more lively.
    * d. all of the above.
       e. none of the above.

16. Which of the following techniques is the most useful for helping members clarify and prioritize their values?
    a. the mirror technique
    * b. the magic shop
    c. the double technique
    d. future projection
    e. the soliloquy

17. Participants can rehearse in a fresh way a course of action with a person they'd like to interact with through which technique?
    a. the mirror technique
    b. the double technique
    * c. future projection
    d. role reversal
    e. presentation of the other

18. The technique whereby a protagonist speaks directly to the audience by expressing some uncensored feeling or thought is:
    a. the mirror technique.
    b. projection.
    * c. soliloquy.
    d. role reversal.
    e. self-presentation.

19. The third phase of a psychodrama consists of:
    * a. sharing what was observed during the action period.
    b. encouraging a protagonist to act out a conflict.
    c. the leader's giving an interpretation of the dynamics of behavior.
    d. some type of nonverbal exercise.

20. Psychodrama is often used in combination with:
    a. behavioral techniques.
    b. psychoanalytic methods.
    c. Gestalt techniques.
    d. encounter group techniques.
    * e. both (c) and (d).

21. Which of the following is *not* a basic concept in psychodrama?
    a. dealing with the present
    b. encounter
    c. lifestyle
    d. family constellation
    * e. both (c) and (d)

22. Psychodrama was designed to facilitate the expression of feelings in a spontaneous and dramatic way through the use of:
    a. free association

* b. role playing.
   c. dream analysis.
   d. nonverbal interaction exercises.
   e. none of the above.

23. Related to the concept of encounter is the term:
    a. spontaneity.
  * b. tele.
    c. creativity.
    d. confrontation.
    e. support.

24. A special characteristic of psychodramatic methods is that they are applicable to:
  * a. almost any theoretical framework.
    b. no other theoretical frameworks.
    c. experiential therapies only.
    d. cognitive and behavioral therapies only.

25. The ventilation of stored-up feelings is known as:
    a. breaking out.
    b. breaking down.
    c. working through.
  * d. catharsis.
    e. acting out.

26. Role-playing techniques have been used by:
    a. psychoanalysts.
    b. Adlerians.
    c. Rogerians (person-centered therapists).
    d. eclectic therapists.
  * e. all of the above.

27. The auxiliary ego typically assumes the function(s) of:
    a. portraying the roles of significant others in the life of the protagonist.
    b. a double for the protagonist in helping him or her verbalize feelings.
    c. directing the course of the psychodrama.
    d. gathering information from the protagonist by using the life assessment form.
  * e. both (a) and (b).

28. The most important issue in the warm-up phase is creating an atmosphere that fosters:
  * a. spontaneity.
    b. specificity of behavioral goals.
    c. a regression to early childhood memories.
    d. an ability to critically evaluate one's thoughts.
    e. none of the above.

29. Role playing can serve the function(s) of being used as a method of:
    a. treatment.
    b. diagnosis.
    c. instruction.
    d. training.
  * e. all of the above.

30. Which of the following is (are) an ethical issue(s) in the practice of psychodrama?
    a. the irresponsible use of psychodramatic procedures.
    b. untrained persons using psychodramatic approaches.
    c. leaders being attracted to psychodrama to fill their own egotistical needs.
    d. romanticizing psychodrama as a single approach.
  * e. all of the above.

CHAPTER 9   THE EXISTENTIAL APPROACH TO GROUPS

Lecture Notes and Outline

I. *Learning Objectives.* When students complete this chapter, they should be able to describe:

   A. The basic concepts that are a part of the existential approach;

   B. The therapeutic goals of this approach, as applied to group work;

   C. How the concepts of this approach can be translated into group practice;

   D. The role and function of the existentially oriented group leader;

   E. The applications of the existential approach to working with family groups; and

   F. The unique contributions and basic limitations of the existential approach to group work.

II. *Key Terms to Identify and Define*
   - experiential approach
   - "third force" in psychology
   - existentialism
   - humanistic emphasis
   - authenticity
   - inauthenticity
   - self-awareness
   - consciousness
   - existential anxiety
   - neurotic anxiety
   - being-in-the-world
   - I-Thou relationship

III. *Lecture Outline: Notes and Comments*
   A. Introduction
      1. In my lecture I stress that this is an *approach* to working with individuals in a group, not a well-defined system or a set of techniques.

2. My emphasis is on the key ideas, as outlined in the chapter in the textbook and *Student Manual*. I present these key concepts as critical factors in group process, and ask students to think about techniques they can borrow from the other therapeutic approaches to translate these concepts into the practice of group work.

B. Key Concepts from the Existential Approach
   1. In addition to the key concepts that I have described in the textbook chapter, I draw heavily on another book that I wrote for material for this lecture/discussion/demonstration/ experiential session. This book is *I Never Knew I Had a Choice.* (sixth edition, 1997). The themes that I take from this book are:
      - autonomy
      - work and the meaning of life
      - love/sex/intimacy
      - sex roles
      - loneliness and solitude
      - death, separation, and loss
      - meaning of life and values
   2. *I Never Knew I Had a Choice, Sixth Edition* is written in such a way that readers are expected to become personally involved with the material, and many experiential exercises are provided. I use the structure and contents of this book for an entire three-day weekend workshop. Students co-lead their own group, each by taking a topic such as loneliness, death and dying, meaning in life, and so forth. These topics can provide excellent catalysts for experiencing the key themes of the existential approach in regular class sessions.
   3. In addition to the above text, an instructor's manual is provided, with many exercises and group activities. *Instructor's Manual* for *I Never Knew I Had a Choice* (Brooks/Cole, 1997) provides detailed self-inventories, group exercises, techniques that can be used in groups, and questions for discussion. If you are interested in student involvement with the concepts described, additional suggested ideas for group work will be found in the *Instructor's Manual*.

C. Key Ideas Applicable to Group Practice
   1. I stress the importance of looking for ways that members might attempt to avoid accepting responsibility for themselves. We discuss in detail the connection between freedom and responsibility, and explore ways that we create our lives.
   2. The concept of ways of expanding self-awareness in groups is given emphasis, along with challenging members to accept the responsibility for action that accompanies this increased awareness.
   3. I ask students to talk about sources of anxiety they experience in making key decisions in their lives. In small groups, they focus

on past decisions and the effects of these decisions on their lives now.
4. This approach accentuates the importance of accepting death as a way of increasing the meaning of life. We do many types of exercises to focus on the reality of death, and to focus on the implications for changing the way we are living.

Focus Questions for Chapter 9: The Existential Approach to Groups
1. The existential approach to group is more of a perspective on human nature and an approach to understanding behavior than a "school of therapy." With this in mind, how does an existential practitioner view group counseling?
2. How are self-awareness, freedom and responsibility, and choosing for oneself *basic goals* of the existential group?
3. What are the implications of the concept of *self-awareness* for group practice?
4. Discuss the implications for the concepts of *self-determination* and *personal responsibility* for group counseling.
5. How does the existential group leader view anxiety? What are the meanings of anxiety?
6. Discuss the existential view of *death* as a significant variable in living fully. How might an existential practitioner focus on this reality in group counseling? How are death and meaning in life related concepts?
7. The existential practitioner speaks about the concept of *authentic identity*. Discuss this concept of authenticity and contrast it with *inauthentic* identity. How do you see this as a significant concept for the practice of group work?
8. How would an existential practitioner view concepts such as loneliness and being alone? In what way might such a practitioner work with these experiences in a group? Discuss both.
9. Discuss the role of the existential group leader. How does this role fit for you?
10. This model does not specify a set of techniques. If you were to borrow existential *concepts* and integrate them into your work as a group leader, how might you draw upon other approaches as a basis of techniques? What other schools might you rely on?
11. Critically evaluate this approach to group counseling. Discuss what you see as its major assets and its major liabilities. How does this approach work with culturally diverse clients?

Quiz: Comprehension Check
Indicate whether each of the following statements is *T* (true) or *F* (false) as it applies to the *existential approach in groups*.

(F) 1. Many existential philosophers spelled out some of the implications of existential philosophy for the practice of group counseling/therapy.
(F) 2. Existential philosophers such as Heidegger and Kierkegaard view anxiety as an indication of "inauthentic existence."
(T) 3. Self-determination, or the capacity to exercise choice in the face of limits, is a key concept of the existential approach.
(F) 4. Philosophically, the existential and the psychoanalytic approaches have a common set of assumptions regarding the nature of the person.
(T) 5. Existential guilt grows from a sense of incompleteness or the realization that we are not becoming the persons we are capable of becoming.
(T) 6. The humanistic psychologists propose that each of us can move toward self-actualization.
(F) 7. The existential approach provides many specific therapeutic techniques to attain the goal of increasing self-awareness, freedom, and responsibility.
(T) 8. The existential approach developed as a reaction to both psychoanalysis and behaviorism.
(T) 9. Humanistic psychology and existential psychology have some relationship since they share some of the same basic tenets and assumptions.
(T) 10. The meaning of death should be examined in group counseling sessions.

Quiz: The Existential Approach to Groups
1. A basic assumption of the existential approach is:
   a. that humans cannot escape from freedom.
   b. that humans tend to be determined by external forces.
   c. that early influences shape and determine the contemporary person.
   d. that with freedom comes responsibility.
   * e. both (a) and (d).

2. Existential therapy is basically:
   a. a set of techniques for group work.
   * b. an approach to group work.
   c. a unified school of therapy.
   d. a combination of most of the other current therapies.
   e. a scientific mode of group work.

3. The basic goal of the existential group is:
   a. to adjust the members to the demands of society.
   b. to expand self-awareness.
   c. to help members accept the responsibility of choosing.
   d. to treat symptoms so that members can be free of existential anxiety.
   * e. both (b) and (c).

4. The existential group focuses on:
* a. here-and-now forces within the group.
   b. unresolved conflicts that have been repressed in childhood.
   c. techniques designed to assist members in gaining catharsis.
   d. measuring the observable outcomes of a group.
   e. the agenda developed by the leader.

5. The implication of self-awareness for group practice is:
   a. that repression is a strong factor in human behavior.
   b. that humans tend to shy away from awareness of themselves.
   c. that awareness of the causes of one's problems provides the key to resolving these problems.
* d. that through self-awareness members are confronted with the responsibility to direct their own lives.
   e. that through self-awareness members will discover that they have a fixed nature.

6. The concept of freedom in the existential approach implies that group members:
   a. are free to be whatever they want to be.
   b. are free without restrictions.
   c. have freedom of options to determine their own destinies.
   d. have the freedom to act or to be acted upon.
* e. both (c) and (d).

7. Within the existential approach, anxiety is viewed as:
   a. a sign that one is ready for change.
   b. a sign of neurotic behavior.
   c. a basic part of being human.
   d. a recognition and acceptance that we are ultimately accountable for how our lives turn out.
* e. two of the above.

8. The existential view of death is:
   a. that it renders us hopeless.
   b. that it makes life less meaningful.
* c. that it gives meaning to every moment.
   d. that it creates an existential vacuum.

9. The function of the existential group leader is:
   a. to understand the member's subjective world.
   b. to explore the member's past history.
   c. to challenge each member to discover alternatives.
   d. none of the above.
* e. both (a) and (c).

10. According to the existential viewpoint:
   a. meaning is automatically given to us by the fact that we are humans.
* b. we must create our own meaning in life.

c. the group leader needs to point out what the meaning of one's life should be.
   d. there is no real meaning to life as the world is meaningless.
   e. meaning is derived from social interest.

11. Authenticity consists of:
    a. making the right choices.
    b. living by the expectations of significant others.
    c. choosing in the face of uncertainty.
    d. taking the stand to define and affirm ourselves.
  * e. both (c) and (d).

12. The central issue(s) in therapy, according to the existential view, is (are):
    a. resistance.
  * b. freedom and responsibility.
    c. transference.
    d. experiencing feelings.
    e. none of the above.

13. According to the existential approach, *guilt* is:
    a. a manifestation of neurotic behavior.
    b. an irrational response.
    c. a form of immaturity.
    d. evidence that we are not fully free or self-actualized.
  * e. none of the above.

14. Groups can be useful for:
    a. dealing with feelings of being alone.
    b. dealing with the fear of making choices.
    c. learning through the struggles of others.
    d. recognizing that each of us must ultimately choose for ourselves.
  * e. all of the above.

15. The role of techniques in the existential group is that:
  * a. techniques should be secondary to understanding members.
    b. techniques are specified to bring about change.
    c. techniques interfere with the therapeutic process.
    d. techniques imply a loss of faith in the client's ability to find his or her own way.

16. Which technique is considered essential in the existential group?
    a. script analysis
    b. role playing
    c. the use of fantasy
    d. free association
  * e. none of the above

17. In an existential group, the leader would tend to:
  * a. challenge members to become aware of their choices.
    b. draw upon highly dramatic group techniques.

c. aim for a catharsis for each group member.
   d. urge members to get rid of guilt and anxiety.
   e. encourage a regression to one's early past.

18. The existential approach comes under the category of which movement?
   * a. the third force
   b. the new wave
   c. insight therapies
   d. cognitive therapies

19. Which of the following is *not* true of anxiety from an existential perspective?
   * a. Anxiety is the root of most neurosis.
   b. Anxiety is "the dizziness of freedom."
   c. Anxiety is a basic characteristic of being human.
   d. Anxiety can often be the catalyst for growth and change.
   e. Not recognizing anxiety can lead to constricting our lives and limiting our choices.

20. Which of the following persons has built a therapeutic approach primarily on the search for meaning?
   a. Carl Rogers
   b. Irving Yalom
   * c. Viktor Frankl
   d. Paul Tillich
   e. Eric Berne

CHAPTER 10   THE PERSON-CENTERED APPROACH TO GROUPS

Lecture Notes and Outline
   I. *Learning Objectives.* At the conclusion of this unit, students are expected to:

   A. Understand the stages of the development of a group within the person-centered perspective;

   B. Define and describe the facilitative dimensions of the therapeutic relationship;

   C. Describe the role and functions of the group counselor within the person-centered context;

   D. Be familiar with the process directions taken by a person-centered group, and to be able to describe the outcomes of such a group; and

   E. Be able to demonstrate the ability to apply the basic concepts of this model to actual group practice.

II. *Key Terms to Identify and Define*
   - empathy
   - unconditional positive regard
   - basic acceptance
   - genuineness or congruence
   - nondirective approach
   - congruence
   - confrontation
   - the formative tendency
   - humanistic psychology
   - client-centered therapy

III. *Lecture Outline: Notes and Comments*
   A. Introduction
      1. I find it helpful to ask students what they know about this approach and what their reactions are to the model. They are alerted to look for specific concepts and techniques in this model that they might incorporate into their own developing style of leading groups—a theme that runs throughout all the class sessions.

   B. Key Concepts in Group Process
      1. Students at times have trouble in actually translating some of the core dimensions into actual group practice. These many concepts (empathy, positive regard, respect, acceptance, warmth, and so on) need to be understood on more than an abstract level.
      2. To make these concepts concrete, we tend to do a lot of experiential work in small groups. Students discuss what might block their degree of caring and regard for clients. The focus in these groups is on the attitudes of the students, and how these attitudes are likely to influence the way in which they lead groups.

   C. Evaluation of Person-Centered Approach
      1. In my lectures I stress that students can take the foundation of this model (emphasis on creating trust and giving the group members responsibility for direction of group) and apply it to other models. At times students think that unless they limit themselves to reflection and clarification, they cannot use this model. My hope is to demonstrate that they can use this model as the groundwork for including some of the more active-directive approaches. If they have not established a climate of trust and concern in a group, then most of the more directive techniques may fail.
      2. Again, emphasis is on actual practice of this model, rather than merely on learning about it through lecture. Students in class form small groups, co-leaders are selected, and their task is to work within the framework of this model as best they can, so that they can evaluate which aspects they might use in the groups they lead.

Focus Questions for Chapter 10: The Person-Centered Approach to Groups

1. List and describe the *basic assumptions* that a person-centered group leader holds regarding human nature and toward the nature of group process.

2. According to the person-centered group leader, what are the *central goals* of group counseling?

3. Define *attending*. How is this a fundamental concept of this approach?

4. What is *empathy*? In what way is this basic to the person-centered group? Discuss the implication of empathy for group leadership.

5. What do you understand by the phrase "unconditional positive regard"? In what way is this a basic part of the person-centered approach?

6. What is the primary role of the group counselor according to this model? Could you function effectively in such a role? Why or why not?

7. Describe the process directions that make up the stages or phases of the person-centered group.

8. What role does research play in this model? What kind of research is stressed?

9. Critically appraise the person-centered model of group work. In your critique mention the aspects that you most like and least like. What aspects of this model would you want to incorporate into your leadership style? What do you see as the main contributions and limitations of this approach?

10. What kind of population do you see as being best suited to a person-centered approach?

Quiz: Comprehension Check

In the space provided place a *T* if you see the answer as true and an *F* if you see the answer as false. Use this quiz to check your general mastery of the chapter. You can also use these statements as discussion material in class.

(F) 1. It is almost impossible to have empathy with a client who has problems you have not experienced yourself.

(T) 2. Empathy is one of the central characteristics needed for effective group work.

(F) 3. Group leaders in this model insist on a contract as a condition to beginning a group.

(T) 4. The attitudes a group counselor holds are more important than his or her knowledge of techniques and skills according to the person-centered approach.

(F) 5. The person-centered model is classified as a form of cognitive, behaviorally oriented therapy.

(T) 6. The person-centered approach is akin to the existential approach in that they share fundamental principles.

(F) 7. The term *congruence* means much the same as the phrase *empathic understanding*.
(F) 8. A good definition of the phrase *unconditional positive regard* is the capacity to see the world of another by assuming the internal frame of reference of another person.
(T) 9. The concept of *immediacy* refers to "you-me" talk or direct and mutual talk between client and therapist.
(F) 10. When a group is moving slowly, Rogers suggests that a group leader make interpretive comments to facilitate the process.

Quiz: The Person-Centered Approach to Groups
1. The basic assumption underlying the person-centered approach is:
    a. that members are prone to faulty thinking.
    b. that members need guidance from an expert to resolve their problems.
    c. that members need a structured learning experience to benefit from a group.
    d. all of the above.
   * e. none of the above.

2. The person-centered approach is a form of:
    a. neo-psychoanalytic therapy.
    b. cognitive-behavior therapy.
   * c. humanistic therapy.
    d. rational therapy.
    e. both (b) and (d).

3. Which of the following would be stressed the most in a person-centered group?
    a. confronting members with early decisions that are no longer appropriate
    b. getting members to involve themselves in fantasy exercises
    c. active listening and responding
    d. empathy
   * e. both (c) and (d)

4. Unconditional positive regard means:
    a. liking everything about the members.
    b. being tolerant of any behaviors in a group.
    c. accepting members despite what they do outside of the group.
    d. feeling a warmth toward every client.
   * e. none of the above.

5. A person-centered group leader is best described as a:
    a. teacher.
    b. friend.
    c. judge.
   * d. facilitator.
    e. expert.

6. Which of the following is considered important in the person-centered approach?
   a. accurate interpretation on the part of the leader
   b. accurate diagnosis and formulation of a treatment plan
   * c. the attitudes of a group leader
   d. analysis of underlying dynamics of behavior
   e. none of the above

7. The crucial factor that determines the outcome of the person-centered group is:
   a. the leader's technical skills.
   * b. the leader's relationship with the members in the group.
   c. the leader's knowledge of group dynamics.
   d. the members' willingness to think rationally.
   e. defining specific and measurable goals.

8. Empathy refers to the group leader's ability to:
   a. like and care for the members.
   b. feel exactly what the members are feeling and to share experiences that are similar to those of the members.
   c. objectively understand the dynamic of a member.
   d. accurately diagnose the core of a member's problem.
   * e. sense accurately the inner world of a member's subjective experience.

9. The *congruence* of a group leader implies:
   a. empathy.
   b. respect.
   c. immediacy.
   * d. genuineness.
   e. unconditional positive regard.

10. Carl Rogers' view of the use of group techniques is that:
    a. planned exercises often interfere with the power of a group to find its own direction.
    b. members should be involved in any exercises that are introduced in the group.
    c. techniques should be used only when members seem lost and when they need leader direction.
    d. techniques can be effective in opening people up to areas that they are resistant to explore.
    * e. both (a) and (b).

11. Which technique(s) is (are) used in the person-centered group?
    a. probing and questioning
    b. interpretation
    c. direct confrontation of games in an aggressive manner
    d. structured communication exercises in groups
    * e. none of the above

12. Which procedure(s) is (are) *not* typically used in a person-centered group?
    a. diagnosis and evaluation
    b. active listening
    c. advice-giving
    d. responding with immediate feelings
    * e. both (a) and (c)

13. What is the position of the person-centered group leader on the use of questioning?
    a. It is useful to ask probing questions.
    b. *What* and *how* questions are more distracting than *why* questions.
    c. Questions are essential to provide direction to a group.
    * d. Questions are generally best avoided.
    e. None of the above.

14. Which of the following would Rogers consider to be the most important in bringing about change?
    * a. empathy
    b. leader skill
    c. accurate interpretations
    d. positive regard

15. What is the value placed by Rogers on research on group process?
    a. It is seen as largely irrelevant.
    b. It is seen as something that should be done with objective measurement.
    c. It is seen as a process that taps the subjective experience of members' views of the group.
    d. It should be an ongoing process.
    * e. Both (c) and (d).

16. The attitudes of leader congruence, accurate empathic understanding, and unpossessive caring are considered by the person-centered approach to be:
    a. necessary but *not* sufficient to effect change.
    b. neither necessary nor sufficient factors of client change.
    * c. both necessary and sufficient factors to effect change within the members.

17. Which of the following is a contribution of the person-centered approach to groups?
    a. It focuses on an objective view of behavior.
    * b. It has relied on research to validate the concepts and practices of this approach.
    c. It has generated a wide range of therapeutic techniques.
    d. It stresses the leader's ability to translate therapy into practice by focusing on the skill development of the leader.
    e. None of the above.

18. Which of the following is *not* considered a key concept of the person-centered approach?
   * a. existential vacuum
   b. congruence
   c. unconditional positive regard
   d. empathic understanding
   e. non-possessive warmth

19. The best definition of empathy is:
   a. to feel pity for the client.
   b. to tell the client that you know what he or she is feeling.
   * c. to sense the private world of the client as if it were your own.
   d. to feel sympathy.

20. The concept of unconditional positive regard is most closely associated with:
   * a. warmth.
   b. trust.
   c. congruence.
   d. genuineness.
   e. both (c) and (d).

CHAPTER 11   GESTALT THERAPY

Lecture Notes and Outline

I. *Learning Objectives.* Upon completing this chapter, students are expected to:

   A. Become familiar with the stages of group development according to the Gestalt perspective;

   B. Acquire a knowledge of the rationale for the Gestalt techniques that are commonly used in group work; and

   C. Understand the basic concepts of Gestalt therapy such as goals, present-centered awareness, responsibility, unfinished business, and so forth.

II. *Key Terms to Identify and Define*
   - unfinished business
   - experiential therapy
   - continuum of awareness
   - impasse
   - the experiment
   - the here and now
   - energy
   - resistance to contact
   - introjection
   - retroflection
   - blocks to energy
   - Gestalt dream work
   - rehearsal technique
   - Gestalt techniques
   - avoidance
   - field theory
   - responsibility
   - boundary disturbance
   - projection
   - confluence

- deflection
- paradoxical theory of change
- organismic self-regulation
- contact
- figure-formation process

III. *Lecture Outline: Notes and Comments*
   A. Introduction
      1. Students generally have an interest in actually experiencing the Gestalt techniques in a group. Thus, I attempt to demonstrate this model in action, and then discuss the rationale for the approach after they have experienced the process.
      2. Tie in this model with the humanistic tradition of the existential approach and with the approach of Carl Rogers. In what ways is Gestalt therapy a form of existential therapy? How is this model particularly appropriate for group interaction?
   B. Key Concepts in Group Process
      1. There are only a few concepts that I stress in a brief lecture, and these include:
         - the goals of Gestalt therapy
         - the concept of present-centered awareness
         - bringing the past and the future into the now
         - experiencing, rather than talking about
         - gaining ongoing awareness of feelings
         - identifying unfinished business from the past
         - stress on *what* and *how*
      2. Each of the above concepts lends itself to practice in a group situation. See the *Student Manual* for numerous suggestions for integrating experience with lecture.
   C. Applications and Techniques
      1. A danger I see with this approach is that beginning students can learn Gestalt techniques as gimmicks, which are sometimes seen as a "bag of tricks." Typically, I encourage students to experiment with these techniques with themselves. They are asked to see what they can learn about themselves by trying certain Gestalt exercises. Most of the content of the *Student Manual* for this chapter deals with these exercises. For example, rather than *talking about* their concerns and personal issues, they are asked to deal with these concerns as though a certain interaction were going on now.
      2. This approach provides plenty of tools for students to apply to themselves in small groups or self-directed groups. They can use the Gestalt exercises as catalysts for their own groups and for working on their personal issues.
      3. I emphasize the importance of using some caution in applying these techniques in the groups they lead. First, they need to experience these techniques *as members*. The techniques that we typically experience in class or group include:

- working with fantasy
- the two-chair technique
- the rehearsal technique
- exaggeration exercises
- experimenting with language approaches
- focus on nonverbal messages
- sentence completion exercises

Focus Questions for Chapter 11: Gestalt Therapy

1. Describe the basic assumptions underlying the Gestalt approach to group work.

2. What are the therapeutic goals of the Gestalt group? Discuss.

3. Discuss the concept of the "here and now" as it relates to Gestalt therapy. How does this approach deal with both the *past* and the *future*?

4. What are some advantages of the Gestalt emphasis on reexperiencing past traumas as though they were occurring in the present?

5. The core of the Gestalt methodology is awareness, or recognizing what one is thinking, feeling, sensing, and doing. How does the Gestalt group leader see this awareness as a crucial and basic part of the therapeutic process?

6. What is the position of the Gestalt leader in using questions?

7. Discuss the concept of *unfinished business* from the Gestalt viewpoint. How would a Gestalt group leader attempt to work with unfinished business in a group? What are some techniques for dealing with unfinished business?

8. Discuss the role and functions of the Gestalt group leader. How comfortable would you be in assuming the role?

9. Discuss the concept of *experiments* designed to expand awareness. How are the various Gestalt techniques really experiments?

10. Do you see a danger of abusing Gestalt techniques? In what way is it essential for the therapist to be genuine if these techniques are to be effective?

11. In what way does the Gestalt approach focus on:
    a. verbal language patterns?
    b. nonverbal communication aspects?

12. Define these Gestalt techniques. Give a concise description of each procedure, along with its purpose.
    a. the dialogue approach
    b. making the rounds
    c. rehearsal
    d. reversal technique
    e. exaggeration exercise

13. How is fantasy used in a Gestalt group? What are some advantages you can see to using fantasy approaches?
14. Discuss how Gestalt therapists work with dreams in a group. Describe the procedures used as well as the rationale.
15. Write a *critique* of the Gestalt approach to groups. Include what you see as its main contributions and strengths, major limitations and weaknesses, the populations especially suited for Gestalt, and the concepts and procedures you'd most want to use from the Gestalt model.

Quiz: Comprehension Check
In the space provided, mark a *T* if the statement is true for the Gestalt orientation or *F* if it is false.

(F) 1. Gestalt leaders typically ask *why* questions.
(F) 2. The focus in a Gestalt group is on an intellectual awareness of one's problems as well as on doing cognitive work to change irrational beliefs.
(T) 3. The Gestalt approach shares with psychodrama the emphasis on emotionally experiencing a conflict in the immediate moment as opposed to simply talking about the conflict.
(F) 4. The Gestalt approach comes under the general category of *behavioral* counseling.
(T) 5. Avoidance is a central concept in the Gestalt approach.
(F) 6. Confluence is a term that refers to having good contact with the environment.
(F) 7. One of the limitations of a Gestalt approach is the emphasis upon cognitive factors and not enough attention to affective aspects.
(F) 8. An aim of the Gestalt group is to help the individual adjust to his or her environment.
(F) 9. In introjection, we disown certain aspects of ourselves by ascribing them to the environment.
(T) 10. A criticism of the Gestalt approach is that meager research has been done to assess its effectiveness.

Quiz: Gestalt Therapy
1. A primary function of the Gestalt leader is to:
   a. make interpretations for the members.
   b. serve as a blank screen to foster transference.
   * c. suggest experiments that will lead to heightening experiencing.
   d. confront clients' irrational thoughts.
   e. help clients modify their life scripts.

2. Gestalt therapy focuses on:
   a. exploration of the past.
   * b. the here and now.
   c. the future.
   d. both the past and the future.

3. Which of the following is *not* a key concept of the Gestalt group?
   a. awareness
   b. unfinished business
   * c. intellectual understanding of one's basic problem
   d. here-and-now focus
   e. dealing with the impasse

4. In Gestalt therapy awareness is best described as:
   a. introspection.
   b. insight.
   * c. recognition of current feelings, actions, and sensations.
   d. recognition of why one struggles with a certain problem.
   e. none of the above.

5. How is the *past* dealt with in Gestalt therapy?
   a. It is not considered crucial and therefore not dealt with.
   b. Clients talk about past issues and experience relief from this discussion.
   c. Members attempt in the group to figure out what caused their present difficulties by analyzing the past.
   * d. The past is brought into the present moment by asking the member to reexperience this past issue as though it were occurring now.
   e. The past is always related to the future.

6. Unfinished business is related to:
   a. feelings of resentment and guilt.
   b. the concept of avoidance.
   c. issues from the past that interfere with present functioning.
   * d. all of the above.
   e. none of the above.

7. Which of the following would a Gestalt group leader probably *not* do?
   a. challenge members to experience whatever blockages and barriers that could prevent full awareness
   b. apply skillful frustration so that members are encouraged to give up ways of being helpless
   c. suggest experiments to be carried out in a group
   d. be self-disclosing in the therapeutic relationship
   * e. a Gestalt leader might well do any of the above

8. Gestalt therapy techniques are designed to assist members to:
   a. contact their present experience more fully.
   b. bring more life to therapeutic interactions.
   c. intensify certain feelings.
   * d. all of the above.
   e. none of the above.

9. The focus of a Gestalt therapy group is on:
   a. free associating to one another's dreams.
   b. understanding why we feel or act as we do.

c. recognizing one's own projections and refusing to accept helplessness.
   d. carrying out experiments that are aimed at intensifying here-and-now awareness.
* e. both (c) and (d).

10. Which experiment(s) is (are) often used in a Gestalt group?
   a. the use of fantasy
   b. working with dreams
   c. asking members to rehearse out loud what they are telling themselves
   d. asking members to engage in dialogue with various sides of themselves
* e. all of the above

11. The Gestalt approach to dreams:
* a. asks the members to discover the meaning the dream has for them.
   b. teaches members the universal meaning of dream symbols.
   c. rests mainly on the skill of the leader in interpreting the dream for the member.
   d. always involves the use of free association.
   e. all of the above.

12. Gestalt experiments are aimed at:
   a. teaching members how to think rationally.
* b. integrating conflicting sides within a member.
   c. teaching clients how to discover causes of future problems.
   d. helping members understand unconscious dynamics.
   e. two of the above.

13. The technique of "making the rounds" can be useful when:
   a. members are practicing a new behavior.
   b. members tend to avoid a facet of experience.
   c. members feel stuck.
   d. members would like to develop more spontaneity.
* e. all of the above.

14. An intervention that is typically used to heighten awareness of both introjections and projections is:
   a. the reversal technique.
   b. the rehearsal technique.
   c. working with dreams.
* d. experiments with dialogues.
   e. none of the above.

15. If a member experienced an internal conflict (such as topdog and underdog), which of the following might be most appropriate?
* a. dialogue technique
   b. rehearsal technique
   c. exaggeration

d. making the rounds
e. focusing on language

16. Which of the following is *not* a key concept of the Gestalt approach?
    * a. family constellation
    b. avoidance
    c. here and now
    d. awareness and responsibility
    e. energy

17. In order to attain present-centered awareness, Gestalt therapy focuses on:
    * a. the surface of behavior.
    b. the deeper reasons for why one behaves in certain ways.
    c. early childhood experiences.
    d. early recollections and memories.
    e. none of the above.

18. Which of the following is *not* a principle of Gestalt therapy theory?
    a. organismic self-regulation
    b. field theory
    c. figure-formation process
    * d. separation-individuation process

19. The process of turning back to ourselves what we would like to do to someone else is known as:
    a. introjection.
    b. projection.
    * c. retroflection.
    d. sublimation.
    e. deflection.

20. The process of uncritically accepting others' beliefs and standards without assimilating them to make them congruent with who we are is known as:
    * a. introjection.
    b. projection.
    c. retroflection.
    d. sublimation.
    e. confluence.

CHAPTER 12   TRANSACTIONAL ANALYSIS

Lecture Notes and Outline
I. *Learning Objectives.* After reading and studying this chapter, the students are expected to:

A. Be able to define and describe the key concepts and terms associated with TA approach;

B. Demonstrate the ability to apply some of the common techniques used in group work;
  C. Describe the role and function of the TA group leader;
  D. Have gained some experience in applying the concepts of TA to themselves in small learning groups; and
  E. Critically evaluate this approach to group work.

II. *Key Terms to Identify and Define*
   - ego states
   - Parent/Adult/Child
   - didactic therapy
   - therapeutic contract
   - stroking (positive and negative)
   - injunctions
   - counter-injunctions
   - early decisions
   - redecisions
   - gender-sensitive therapy
   - rackets
   - life script analysis
   - games
   - basic psychological positions
   - life scripts
   - structural analysis
   - transactional analysis
   - game analysis

III. *Lecture Outline: Notes and Comments*
   A. Introduction
      1. I present this approach as one that can be fruitfully combined with Gestalt approaches *and* with some of the cognitive and behavioral approaches. Thus, we relate TA concepts to some of the techniques used in Gestalt, rational emotive behavior therapy, and the behavioral therapies.
      2. It is easy to get lost in the terminology of TA, and thus at the outset I caution students to beware of simply picking up the jargon.
   B. Some Concepts for Discussion and Class Practice
      1. The ego states. What are these ego states, and how can they be identified in a group?
      2. Stroking. Stroking is defined and students have opportunities to experience asking for strokes. The aim of experiential group work in this area is to increase the students' awareness of the kinds of strokes they give others and themselves and to help them ask for the strokes they want.
      3. Injunctions. See the *Student Manual* for a list of common injunctions and an exercise that we often use when we are demonstrating the TA group. This is fairly easy to do in groups, and it generally produces interest in the participants.
      4. Decisions and redecisions. A good follow-up to the concept of parental messages and injunctions are the topics of: What early decisions did you make based on the messages you heard? How do you think these decisions have affected you now? What new decisions might you want to make?

5. The topics of injunctions and decisions, along with the rackets and games we use to support our early decisions, make excellent group material. The *Student Manual* provides material that can be used for experiential group work. As with most of the therapies, TA is used as a catalyst for encouraging students to explore their own development and current conflicts.
6. Besides some work with rackets and games, the students are actually encouraged to do some work with basic life positions that they have incorporated as a part of their personality. By this time, students are better known to one another, and feedback can be useful in relation to what is observed in the group work in class.

Focus Questions for Chapter 12: Transactional Analysis
1. TA provides options for working with family groups on a cognitive, affective, and behavioral level. Show how the concepts of TA can be applied to family members on all these levels. What kinds of TA techniques might you draw upon if you were counseling a family group? Show how you might go about getting a contract from individual family members and the family as a unit.

2. In what sense is TA largely a didactic and cognitive form of therapy?

3. Briefly describe the functioning of the ego states of Parent, Adult, and Child. Show how these concepts are worked with in a group setting.

4. How can a group be a place where people can learn about the kinds of strokes they give and receive?

5. List a few common injunctions. If you were a group leader, how might you explore these injunctions in your group? Describe some techniques for dealing with injunctions.

6. Discuss the concepts of *early decisions* and *redecisions*. In a TA group, how are these early decisions one makes typically explored?

7. As a group leader, what value do you see in exploring games in a group setting? How is a TA group structured in such a way that the members can explore both games and basic psychological positions?

8. Discuss the role and functions of the TA group leader.

9. How do *contracts* guide the direction of work in a group? What are your reactions to the use of contracts in a group?

10. Write a critical evaluation of TA. What specific aspects, both concepts and procedures, might you want to incorporate from TA into your group leading?

Quiz: Comprehension Check
In the space provided, put a *T* if the statement is true within the framework of TA, or put an *F* if the statement does not apply to this approach.

(T) 1. The Parent ego state consists of *both* the Critical Parent and the Nurturing Parent.
(F) 2. The Parent ego state functions largely as a data processor, computing possible decisions made on the basis of information.
(F) 3. A *racket* is defined as the parent messages that we uncritically incorporate into our Adult ego state.
(T) 4. TA is primarily designed as a form of group treatment, and a group setting is preferable to individual counseling.
(T) 5. Group members should be taught to examine decisions they made early in life and determine if these decisions are still appropriate.
(T) 6. TA is an interactional therapy grounded on the assumption that we make current decisions based on past premises.
(T) 7. The unpleasant feelings that people experience after a game are known as *rackets*.
(F) 8. The Gouldings favor long-term therapy, since they are convinced that clients can make redecisions only if they are committed to years of group therapy.
(F) 9. Although TA is designed to develop both emotional and intellectual awareness, the focus is clearly on the emotional aspects.
(F) 10. Structural analysis is a tool by which members become aware of early traumatic situations that now prevent them from changing.

Quiz: Transactional Analysis
1. Which of the following concepts or processes is *not* associated with TA?
   a. a didactic approach
   b. a cognitive approach
   c. a contractual approach
   * d. a form of the psychoanalytic approach
   e. an interactional approach

2. Which of the following is *not* a key concept of TA?
   a. strokes
   b. rackets
   * c. free association
   d. scripts
   e. games

3. The TA group leader functions as:
   a. a trainer.
   b. a teacher.
   c. a resource person.
   * d. all of the above.
   e. none of the above.

4. Which ego state is the "processor of information"?
   a. Parent
   * b. Adult
   c. Child

5. The founder of transactional analysis is:
   a. Robert Goulding.
 * b. Eric Berne.
   c. J. L. Moreno.
   d. Fritz Perls.
   e. Claude Steiner.

6. The part of the personality that consists of feelings, impulses, and spontaneous reactions is the:
   a. Parent.
   b. Adult.
 * c. Child.

7. According to TA theory, *strokes* are:
   a. necessary only for highly dependent people.
 * b. necessary for healthy development.
   c. needed for children, but not for adults.
   d. needed only in times of crisis.

8. Messages that are given from the Child ego state of the parents is the definition of:
   a. rackets.
 * b. injunctions.
   c. counter-injunctions.
   d. scripts.
   e. games.

9. Messages that come from the Parent ego state of the parents are known as:
   a. rackets.
   b. injunctions.
 * c. counter-injunctions.
   d. scripts.
   e. games.

10. Eric Berne's position was that people were:
    a. driven by irrational forces.
  * b. to a large degree victims of their injunctions.
    c. primarily free to make new decisions.
    d. determined by genetic influences.

11. Collections of bad feelings that people use to justify their life script are known as:
    a. basic decisions.
  * b. rackets.
    c. games.
    d. counter-injunctions.
    e. none of the above.

12. According to Robert and Mary Goulding, people:
    a. are victims of the messages given to them by their parents.

b. are scripted in a passive way.
 * c. have a role in accepting certain messages as children.
   d. have very few real choices.

13. The Gouldings stress which of the following in their group practice?
    a. life scripts
  * b. redecision
    c. analysis of early childhood fixations
    d. transference
    e. none of the above

14. An ongoing series of complementary ulterior transactions progressing to a well-defined, predictable outcome is the definition of:
    a. rackets.
  * b. games.
    c. early decisions.
    d. scripts.
    e. pastimes.

15. According to TA, a *contract* by group members:
    a. should be decided by the leader.
    b. once decided should not be revised.
    c. is an essential place to begin a group.
    d. can be made in steps and is subject to change.
  * e. both (c) and (d).

16. The process by which people become aware of the content and functioning of their ego states of Parent, Adult, and Child is known as:
    a. transactional analysis.
    b. dream analysis.
  * c. structural analysis.
    d. functional analysis.
    e. life script analysis.

17. Transactional analysis is best suited for:
    a. individual counseling.
  * b. group counseling.
    c. work with regressed psychotics.
    d. work only with highly functioning people.

18. In the Gouldings' approach to TA in a group, they sometimes draw upon techniques from which approach?
    a. Gestalt
    b. behavior therapy
    c. psychodrama
    d. family therapy
  * e. all of the above

19. The leader(s) of the *redecisional school* of TA is (are):
    a. Erv and Miriam Polster.
  * b. Robert and Mary Goulding.

  c. Eric Berne.
  d. Claude Steiner.
  e. Muriel James and Dorothy Jongeward.

20. Which of the following is *not* a basic part of the classical Bernian TA approach?
  a. structural analysis
  b. transactional analysis
* c. redecisional therapy
  d. game analysis
  e. life-script analysis

CHAPTER 13 BEHAVIORAL GROUP THERAPY

Lecture Notes and Outline

I. *Learning Objectives.* At the conclusion of this unit, the students are expected to:

  A. Identify the unique characteristics of behavior therapy;

  B. Describe the role and function of the behaviorally oriented group leader;

  C. Describe the stages of development of a behavioral group from the initial stages through the final and follow-up stages;

  D. Describe the multimodal approach to group work;

  E. Be able to describe the nature and purpose of assertion groups, and to summarize the philosophy that underlies assertion training;

  F. Describe the nature of behavioral groups directed toward self-control; and

  G. Critically evaluate both the unique contributions and the limitations of this approach to group work.

II. *Key Terms in This Chapter.* Students are expected to define and describe the following terms as they are related to behavior therapy in group work:

- behavior rehearsal
- assertion training
- learning theory
- contingency contracts
- self-monitoring
- contracts
- the buddy system
- coaching
- feedback
- self-reinforcement
- systematic desensitization
- cognitive behavior modification
- assessment strategies
- treatment program
- cognitive restructuring
- action-oriented methods
- homework assignments
- positive reinforcement
- self-directed change
- target behaviors

- shaping
- modeling
- problem solving
- stress inoculation
- behavioral assessment
- technical eclecticism
- social skills group

- social learning theory
- outcome research
- coping-skills techniques
- multimodal group therapy
- multimethod group approach
- stress management training

III. *Lecture Outline: Notes and Comments*
   A. Introduction
      1. This approach generates a wide range of specific techniques designed for behavioral change. My emphasis is on learning these techniques, along with the rationale for them, so that these action-oriented methods can become a part of the leadership style of the students.
      2. Sometimes students approach this model with both negative feelings and misconceptions. I've found that some students view this approach as "cold and rigid"; I believe, however, that students can apply many of the methods of this model in a flexible manner. At the outset we work on the attitudes students have toward the model.
   B. Some Aspects for Lecture/Discussion and Practice
      1. Students are asked to set up a behavioral group after reading and studying the chapter. This includes thinking about matters such as specific goals, getting baseline data on certain behaviors, doing some form of assessment, and developing a treatment program in group. This setting up of the group is an exercise to be completed in small groups.
      2. Because it is relatively easy to demonstrate, we typically form an assertion training group, which allows for a demonstration of the behavioral techniques. The students are asked to decide on a situation or situations in which they'd like to function more assertively, and from this base we form a demonstration group in abbreviated form. This allows for a clarification and actual experience with specific techniques commonly used in assertion training.
      3. We discuss the differences between behavioral role playing and the type of role playing done in Gestalt, psychodrama, and other experiential approaches.
      4. Modeling is a concept that is accented. Students are asked to think about what behaviors they model for the members of their groups. We talk about the power of teaching by modeling.
      5. A value of this approach is on the specificity of goals. Students get practice in defining goals of their own that they'd like to pursue if they were members of an ongoing group. Typically, students have difficulty in translating broad goals into concrete goals. Small group work, with this as a focus, gives them

practice in making general/global goals as specific as possible. If they have had practice in doing this for themselves, hopefully they will be better able to assist the members of their groups in defining working goals.
6. The *Student Manual* and the chapter in the textbook discuss the specifics of developing a self-directed program. This can be done as an adjunct to group work. Typically, I ask students to work in small groups and work out a program of self-directed change for some behavior they'd like to either increase or decrease.
7. One of the unique contributions of the behavioral approach is its focus on ongoing assessment and evaluation of the process and outcomes of groups. This is stressed in the lecture as something that can be done with any approach. Students are expected to develop some procedures for assessing the gains being made in the group. We discuss these procedures in class.
8. The transfer of learning from the group situation to everyday life is one of the most important aspects of group work. Typically, group leaders do poorly at developing strategies for helping members maximize their gains and think of ways to actually put to use what they have learned in group. The students get practice in thinking of ways to work with groups during the final stages of development. I emphasize in lecture some of the following techniques:
- the use of the buddy system
- using contracts
- developing specific homework assignments
- doing much behavioral rehearsal
- developing a reinforcement system
- discussing possible setbacks in daily life and how to deal with them
- practicing in group desired changes
- much use of constructive feedback

Focus Questions for Chapter 13: Behavior Therapy in Groups
1. Describe the unique characteristics of behavior therapy in groups. What are the areas of focus in this approach to groups?
2. Give a description of the stages in the development of behavior-therapy groups from the initial stages to termination and follow-up.
3. Discuss the emphasis on *cognitive behavior modification*. How are beliefs worked in with the hope that behaviors will change?
4. In what way is assessment (or evaluation) an ongoing and vital part of the behavioral group?
5. Give a rationale for the focus on concrete goals and overt behavior in a behavioral group. Why are specific goals needed?

6. What is the role and function of the behaviorally oriented group leader? How does this apply to you?

7. What are some of the assumptions underlying the multimodal approach to group therapy? What are some ways that this approach differs from other types of behavioral groups?

8. Discuss the philosophy of assertion training. What are its basic goals?

9. If you were to design an assertion training group, what would the key elements of this group be? Describe how you would set up such a group, some of the procedures you would be likely to use, and some of the steps you would take in conducting such a group.

10. Assume that you were interested in designing a self-directed change program, utilizing a group format. Describe some of the steps that would be involved in a group for self-help.

11. In what way does a behavioral group differ fundamentally from a psychoanalytic group?

12. Discuss the concept of activity and action-oriented methods that are part of a behavioral group. You might include techniques such as homework, group practice, behavioral role playing, and so on.

13. Write a critical evaluation of behavioral groups, indicating what you consider to be the major contributions and limitations of this approach. What are some specific behavioral approaches that you'd want to use?

Quiz: Comprehension Check
In the space provided put a *T* if the statement is true for the behavioral perspective or put an *F* if it is false.

(F) 1. Techniques derived from the behavior model cannot be incorporated into the style of an existential group leader.
(F) 2. Before people can make behavioral changes, it is essential that they change certain *attitudes* first.
(F) 3. Behavior therapy is generally a long-term method of treatment.
(T) 4. An assumption of the behavioral orientation is that the behaviors clients express *are* the problem and not merely symptoms of the problem.
(F) 5. Baseline data is information about a client's past functioning.
(F) 6. Contingency contracts are used more with adults than with children.
(T) 7. As a part of problem-solving training, modeling and coaching are often used.
(T) 8. Multimodal group therapy takes into consideration the whole person.
(T) 9. Multimodal group therapy allows for the incorporation of diverse techniques.
(T) 10. Multimodal therapy demands flexibility in the use of techniques.

Quiz: Behavior Therapy in Groups

1. Which is *not* a characteristic of behavior therapy in groups?
    a. focus of a self-managed lifestyle
    b. focus on specific behaviors
    c. a cognitive approach
    * d. a psychodynamic approach
    e. use of action-oriented methods

2. The newer thinking in behavior therapy emphasizes:
    a. cognitive factors.
    b. emotional factors.
    c. social processes.
    d. learning process.
    * e. all of the above.

3. What is (are) the characteristic(s) of the behavioral approach in groups?
    a. a focus on overt and specific behavior
    b. precise therapeutic goals
    c. developing a treatment plan and evaluation of this plan
    d. use of action-oriented methods
    * e. all of the above

4. In a behaviorally oriented group, the decision to use certain techniques to change behavior is based on:
    a. the group leader's therapeutic style.
    b. the desires of the group members.
    * c. the demonstrated effectiveness of the technique.
    d. the theoretical views of the leader.
    e. none of the above.

5. Which is (are) true of the application of behavioral techniques in a group?
    * a. These techniques remain under continual evaluation.
    b. They are experiential in nature.
    c. They are designed to produce insight.
    d. They are usually aimed at catharsis.
    e. All of the above.

6. If people want and expect change, the behavioral group leader contends that it is important that:
    a. they explore the past roots of a particular problem.
    b. they gain insight into the causes of a problem.
    c. they engage in detailed introspection.
    * d. they take specific actions to effect change.
    e. all of the above.

7. Which of the following goals would be most characteristic of a behavioral group?
    a. to tap unconscious processes
    b. to integrate polarities within an individual

c. to help members acquire insight into causes of problems
d. to provide members with an awareness of the ego state they are functioning in
* e. to eliminate or acquire a certain behavior

8. Which of the following techniques is *not* considered a behavioral technique?
   a. self-instruction
 * b. the empty-chair technique
   c. cognitive restructuring
   d. self-reinforcement
   e. thought stopping

9. What is the function of the behavioral leader?
   a. to provide modeling for the client
   b. to assess specific behavioral problems
   c. to provide feedback and reinforcement for members
   d. to apply his or her knowledge of behavioral principles and skills in the resolution of problems
 * e. all of the above

10. Which of the following is *not* a behavioral technique?
    a. contingency contracts
  * b. analysis and interpretation of dreams
    c. modeling
    d. relaxation training
    e. behavior rehearsal

11. Which of the following would be a part of the early stages of a behavioral group?
    a. building of cohesiveness
    b. identifying problematic behavior
    c. assessment
    d. developing baseline data
  * e. all of the above

12. Which of the following is generally a part of the working phase of the behavioral group?
    a. reinforcement
    b. behavioral rehearsal
    c. cognitive restructuring
    d. the buddy system
  * e. all of the above

13. A *primary* concern during the final stages of the behavioral group is:
  * a. promoting transfer of learning.
    b. developing a therapeutic contract.
    c. role-playing various situations.
    d. establishing baseline data.
    e. providing relaxation-training methods.

14. Which of the following techniques is generally *not* associated with the assertion training group?
    a. cognitive restructuring
    * b. life script questionnaire
    c. coaching
    d. discrimination learning
    e. homework

15. Contingency contracts:
    a. are used in family therapy.
    b. are used more often with children than adults.
    c. are used more often with adults than children.
    d. do not specify a time period for performing a desired behavior.
    * e. both (a) and (b).

16. The effect of modeling can be enhanced by:
    a. behavior rehearsal.
    b. coaching.
    c. group feedback.
    * d. all of the above.
    e. none of the above.

17. The process of identifying and evaluating one's cognitions, understanding the negative impact of thinking on behavior, and learning more appropriate self-messages is known as:
    a. stress-inoculation training.
    * b. cognitive restructuring.
    c. reframing.
    d. behavioral alignment.
    e. problem solving.

18. A basic assumption underlying multimodal group therapy is:
    a. that the therapist must be effective as a person.
    b. that therapists need a range of skills and techniques to deal with a range of problems.
    c. that therapists must have "technical eclecticism."
    * d. all of the above.
    e. none of the above.

19. Which of the following is *not* one of the modalities of human functioning in the multimodal approach?
    a. imagery
    * b. spirituality
    c. interpersonal
    d. drugs
    e. affect

20. Which of the following statements is *false* as it is applied to the multimodal approach to group therapy?
    a. Leaders function as trainers, educators, consultants, and role models.

      b. Leaders provide information, instruction, and feedback.
*   c. Leaders avoid using techniques.
      d. Leaders offer constructive criticism and suggestions.
      e. Leaders are appropriately self-disclosing.

CHAPTER 14   RATIONAL EMOTIVE BEHAVIOR THERAPY IN GROUPS

Lecture Notes and Outline

I. *Learning Objectives.* After reading and studying this chapter, students are expected to have a fundamental understanding of the basic concepts of REBT and of the techniques applied in group work. Specific objectives include:

    A. To define and describe the ABC theory of personality and to explain the REBT approach to the origins of behavioral problems;

    B. To list the common irrational beliefs and to develop some methods of confronting these beliefs; and

    C. To critically evaluate the model and determine a basis for selecting certain concepts and procedures in one's group leadership style.

II. *Key Terms to Identify and Define*
- irrational beliefs
- rational-emotive imagery
- homework assignments
- cognitive behavioral
- shame-attacking exercises
- coping self-statements
- ABC theory
- self-indoctrination
- didactic methods
- self-rating
- *must*urbation
- cognitive homework

III. *Lecture Outline: Notes and Comments*
    A. Introduction
        1. I introduce this model and note that some of the concepts of this cognitively oriented and active-directive approach can be fruitfully combined with some of the experiential and relationship-oriented therapies. I find the cognitive and action-oriented methods of value, especially when some merger is developed with models such as Gestalt and psychodrama.
        2. I emphasize the value of combining a cognitive perspective with those therapies that stress exploration of feelings.
        3. I clarify the origins of emotional disturbance according to Ellis. Ellis maintains that self-defeating beliefs are supported and maintained by negative and illogical statements that we make to ourselves over and over. I attempt to get students to think of how this concept applies to their own personal problems.

B. Key Concepts in Group Process
   1. I have students analyze the origin of one of their own core irrational beliefs, using the ABC approach. In small groups, they are asked to discuss certain irrational beliefs that give them problems, and eventually to determine ways that they could confront and change them.
   2. In the *Student Manual* there is a self-inventory of irrational beliefs that I've used as a catalyst for group work. I ask that the students keep a record of their "shoulds" and "musts" for a week or so. This kind of class, particularly at this point in the course, gives ample opportunities to practice new behaviors (both in the class and outside).
   3. Methods of teaching members rational thoughts are discussed and then are actually practiced. As a guide, I use some self-help books written by Ellis.
   4. I show students the ways that REBT is an educational model. We talk about the role of the therapist as a teacher and the importance of an active learning stance on the part of the members.
C. Some Applications of Techniques in the REBT Group
   1. I mention the rationale for using groups with the REBT model, which is mentioned both in the textbook and the *Student Manual*.
   2. We discuss the role and functions of the REBT group leader. This kind of leader must be willing to use active-directive techniques, including confrontation. Ellis claims that REBT techniques are best carried out in an active-directive manner with the role of the leader as being a teacher. I ask students how comfortable they would feel in working within this model. I also emphasize that they can do effective REBT group work in a manner that is different from the style of Albert Ellis. Indeed, an REBT therapist can be gentle and supportive, and at the same time be challenging and use directive methods.
   3. We demonstrate methods of disputing and teaching, then students are given a chance in small self-directed groups to apply this disputation to themselves and attempt to work on some of the irrational elements that lead to problems. I frequently do a demonstration group in which I ask students to identify one of their beliefs that they consider to be irrational. In this group demonstration I typically focus on cognitive methods such as disputing and debating of their dysfunctional thinking. I frequently invite them to design some kind of homework that they would be willing to carry out for a period of at least a week.
   4. Like the behavioral approach, REBT lends itself to actual role-playing practice. I think that the techniques are best taught by demonstration, followed by an opportunity to experience them

in small groups. Thus, we do a fair bit of role-playing with homework assignments as a part of the group work. At the following session, we follow up to see how people did.
5. I focus on describing and demonstrating through role-playing the major cognitive methods that are used in REBT. A few of these techniques that are highlighted include: teaching people how to identify their *shoulds, oughts,* and *musts;* teaching some common ways to dispute self-defeating beliefs; providing examples of coping self-statements instead of negative self-talk; giving examples of cognitive homework; and providing examples of the ways in which humor can be used to expose one's exaggerated thinking that gets one into trouble.
6. In class, I also demonstrate a few REBT emotive techniques that are appropriate for group work. Rational-emotive imagery, shame-attacking exercises, and REBT role playing are especially interesting to demonstrate and then to discuss. Students can be asked to devise a shame-attacking exercise that they might carry out. However, it is well to discuss potential disadvantages of using certain emotive techniques. I spend considerable time in talking about cautions in implementing some of the more powerful REBT techniques.
7. You might want to demonstrate some common behavioral strategies that would be appropriate in REBT groups. Students can be asked to devise behavioral homework that they would be willing to carry out.

D. Evaluation of Rational Emotive Behavior Therapy in Groups
1. Ask students to identify specific concepts and techniques of REBT that they particularly value and would like to use in their groups.
2. REBT has certain advantages in cross-cultural group situations. Students can be asked to discuss ways that they could challenge clients from a different culture, and at the same time maintain an attitude of respect toward different cultural values. Students might discuss any limitations they might see in using REBT group therapy for ethnic-minority clients.
3. I typically ask students to come up with what they consider to be the major strength and the major limitation of REBT as it is applied to group counseling.
4. Ellis does not emphasize a warm and personal relationship between members and the leader. Students can be asked to evaluate the importance of the personal relationship as a factor in building trust within the group.

Note to the instructor: As an exercise, you may want to reproduce this self-inventory of irrational beliefs and use it in small groups as a catalyst for exploring the concept of belief systems in REBT.

Self-Inventory of Irrational Beliefs

Albert Ellis has developed a list of irrational beliefs, which he calls "musturbatory ideologies." The following self-inventory is a modification of some of the key irrational beliefs along with major sub-ideas. Respond to the following statements with T (true) if the statement applies to you and F (false) if the statement does not.

_____ 1. I prefer to avoid facing life's difficulties rather than develop the self-discipline to face reality.

_____ 2. Unless things go the way I want them to, quickly and easily, I get extremely upset.

_____ 3. Unless I find ideal solutions to my problems, the results are catastrophic.

_____ 4. I must win almost everyone's approval, or else I feel like a worthless person.

_____ 5. If I do not prove myself to be thoroughly competent in everything I do, then life becomes unbearable.

_____ 6. I have no right to question the beliefs of those in authority, and I *must* have their approval.

_____ 7. I *must* be loved by those who are significant in my life if I am to survive.

_____ 8. To function adequately, I must have a high degree of certainty in the world.

_____ 9. If I make a mistake, then I deserve to feel guilty and rotten.

_____ 10. Others must treat me with kindness and consideration, and if they don't, they should be blamed and punished for their inconsiderateness.

_____ 11. I should always be perfect, and I deserve to feel guilty whenever I fail to measure up to perfection.

_____ 12. I am afraid to make contact with others because if they were to reject me I'd be devastated.

_____ 13. If justice does not always prevail, then life seems almost too unbearable to continue.

_____ 14. I should expect that I can change my life situation without really working hard at doing so.

_____ 15. I must continually rate myself, and be a severe self-critic, for if I don't then I'll never really accomplish a thing.

Some Suggestions of Things to Do with This Inventory

1. List any other *musts* and *demands* that govern your life. What are some other irrational beliefs that you live by?

a. _____

b. _____

c. _____

d. _____

e. _____

f. _____

2. Go back to the list of "musturbatory ideologies" and circle two or three core irrational beliefs that most influence your thinking, feelings, and behavior. Refer to the textbook where the ABC system of analyzing irrational beliefs is described. Apply this to a critical analysis of these statements you tell yourself.

3. In your group, each of you can select a core belief and present to the group *where* and *how* you incorporated it. The other members of the group can challenge you to produce data to support your assumption. Discuss what you think you get from clinging to certain irrational beliefs. How do you imagine your life would be different if you were to be free of these irrational beliefs?

4. Keep a record for a week or so of situations where you tell yourself that you *must* or *should* do something in order to avoid dire results. The purpose of this explicit recordkeeping is to make you aware of ways that you may be *driven* by unrealistic demands, and how you irrationally assume that, unless you live up to these "shoulds" and "musts," your are worthless and will suffer catastrophic outcomes.

Focus Questions for Chapter 14: Rational Emotive Behavior Therapy in Groups

1. Describe the ABC theory of REBT, and show how emotional-behavioral disorders originate.

2. What is a rationale for the highly directive and confrontational nature of REBT?

3. Do you see that REBT necessarily lends itself to an approach that imposes the leader's values on the members? Discuss.

4. What are some unique advantages of a group setting in practicing REBT? How can the group itself be useful in assisting people to confront and effectively deal with irrational ideas?

5. Discuss the role of homework assignments in the REBT group.

6. REBT is basically an educational model in group work. What are some key aspects that the leader tends to teach the participants?

7. Discuss the role and functions of the REBT group leader. How comfortable would you be in assuming this role? Explain.

8. In what ways does the REBT group build on behavior concepts and incorporate many of the techniques of the behavioral approach? Discuss.

9. Do you see possibilities of integrating the cognitive approach of REBT with some of the more experiential group approaches such as Gestalt therapy? Discuss.

10. Write a critique of REBT, including special mention of aspects of the model that you most like and least like.

Quiz: Comprehension Check
Indicate whether each of the following statements is *T* (true) or *F* (false) as it applies to rational emotive behavior therapy in groups.

(F) 1. REBT is primarily an experiential therapy that focuses on feelings.
(T) 2. Group members need to be taught how to think logically and give themselves new sentences if they hope to change.
(F) 3. Transference plays a significant role in the REBT group.
(T) 4. Marathon group sessions are frequently scheduled as a supplement to regular ongoing REBT group sessions.
(T) 5. Recent modifications of REBT include the addition of behavioral techniques such as imagery methods, relaxation, and flooding.
(F) 6. REBT is based on the assumption that we have an innate tendency toward rational thinking.
(T) 7. The rational emotive behavioral approach does not consider the nature of the relationship between therapist and client as vitally important to the outcomes of the process.
(T) 8. Group members are taught to use logical analysis as a way of undermining their faulty premises.
(T) 9. REBT group leaders tend to be active and directive.
(T) 10. The goals of an REBT group include incorporating a new and more realistic philosophy of life.

Quiz: Rational Emotive Behavior Therapy in Groups
1. According to REBT, people develop psychological disturbances because of:
    a. a traumatic event.
    b. failure to receive love from significant others.
    * c. their belief about certain events.
    d. unfinished business from their past.
    e. inadequate bonding with the mother.

2. According to Ellis, people become emotionally disturbed because:
    a. they continue to indoctrinate themselves with erroneous ideas.
    b. they create this disturbance by accepting certain beliefs.
    c. situations cause stress, leading to a breakdown of defenses.
    d. unconscious factors militate against effective functioning.
    * e. both (a) and (b).

3. In the REBT group, members are concerned about:
    a. understanding the origins of their emotional disturbances.
    b. understanding the problems of other members.
    c. freeing themselves of their symptoms.
    d. minimizing ways they create their own disturbances.
    * e. all of the above.

4. REBT can best be considered:
   a. an educational method.
   b. a didactic process.
   c. the process of challenging ideas and thinking.
   d. a teaching-learning process.
   * e. all of the above.

5. REBT methodology includes all of the following procedures except:
   a. confrontation.
   b. logical analysis.
   * c. analysis of transference.
   d. counter-propaganda.
   e. behavioral methods.

6. Which of the following is (are) *not* generally associated with the REBT group?
   a. self-rating
   b. information giving
   c. homework assignments
   * d. analysis of rackets
   e. role playing

7. A REBT group leader is interested in:
   a. creating a climate in a group where members can reenact unfinished business from their past.
   * b. showing members how they have created their own misery.
   c. helping members resolve transference relationships within the group.
   d. assisting members to fully experience whatever they are feeling in the present moment.

8. The REBT group leader assumes that people's illogical beliefs:
   a. are easily changed once the person sees they are illogical.
   b. are the result of activating events that cause certain emotional disturbances.
   * c. are so deeply ingrained that they will not change easily.
   d. are caused by lack of love from parents.
   e. are something we cannot change.

9. In the REBT group, homework assignments are:
   a. carried out in the group.
   b. carried out in daily life.
   c. seen as basic to the REBT method.
   d. a way to practice new behavior.
   * e. all of the above.

10. In REBT, role playing:
    a. is rarely done.
    b. is of a strictly cognitive nature.
    c. is designed to evoke intense feelings.

* d. involves a cognitive-emotive evaluation of feelings and beliefs.
  e. involves a member acting out all the various roles of a present conflict.

11. In the REBT group, role playing:
    a. involves a cognitive restructuring of attitudes.
    b. involves learning through modeling and imitation.
    c. typically involves a cognitive analysis.
    d. is often combined with other behavioral procedures.
  * e. all of the above.

12. Members of an REBT group learn how to:
    a. confront irrational philosophies.
    b. tap unconscious dynamics.
    c. interpret the meaning of their dreams.
    d. develop social skills.
  * e. both (a) and (d).

13. The role of the REBT group leader can be best characterized as:
  * a. a didactic and highly directive role.
    b. a facilitator.
    c. an I-Thou model of relating.
    d. a blank screen that receives projections.
    e. both (b) and (d).

14. REBT groups are primarily aimed at:
    a. removing disabling symptoms.
    b. providing a warm and accepting atmosphere.
    c. challenging self-defeating patterns of thought and action.
    d. challenging one's philosophy of life.
  * e. both (c) and (d).

15. Which of the following is (are) the advantage(s) of using REBT in a group setting?
    a. The group serves as a laboratory where the behavior of members can be directly observed in action.
    b. Multiple transferences are more apt to occur in a group.
    c. Members can get feedback and challenge from others in a group.
    d. Members can free associate with one another's dreams.
  * e. Both (a) and (c).

16. REBT groups often use which procedures?
    a. assertion-training methods
    b. didactic teaching methods
    c. homework assignments
    d. audio-video presentations
  * e. all of the above

17. REBT belongs to which general category of theory?
    a. psychodynamic
    b. client-centered and experientially oriented

  c. existential
* d. cognitive-behavior-action oriented
  e. relationship-oriented

18. According to REBT, change will come about:
   * a. mainly by a commitment to consistently practice new behaviors that challenge old and ineffective ones.
    b. only when we discover the source of our problems.
    c. generally after we relive a traumatic situation in therapy and work through the impasse that prevents new growth.
    d. by awareness itself.
    e. when significant others give us what we expect from them.

19. Feelings of anxiety, depression, rejection, anger, and guilt are initiated and perpetuated by:
    a. unfortunate events that happen to us.
   * b. a self-defeating belief system.
    c. a significant person in our life who rejects us.
    d. a faulty life script.
    e. parental demands during one's childhood.

20. The group leader is likely to begin a group by:
    a. asking the members to complete the life-script checklist.
    b. using nonverbal exercises to build trust.
   * c. teaching members REBT's ABC theory.
    d. using direct and confrontive techniques to undermine the members' irrational thinking.
    e. creating a climate of warmth and empathy.

CHAPTER 15 REALITY THERAPY IN GROUPS

Lecture Notes and Outline

I. *Learning Objectives.* After reading and studying this chapter, the students are expected to have a basic grasp of the key concepts of reality therapy as applied to a group. Other specific objectives include:

 A. To understand how success identity, emphasis on present behavior, self-evaluation, and making a commitment to change behavior are each a basic part of reality therapy;

 B. To understand how choice theory operates and how everything that we do, think, and feel is generated by what happens inside of us;

 C. To explore Glasser's perspective of total behavior which states that to understand our behavior we must take into account what we are doing, thinking, feeling, and our physiological states;

 D. To examine the role and functions of the reality-therapy group leader;

E. To become familiar with the practice of reality therapy in groups, which is known as the "cycle of counseling," and which includes two major components—the counseling environment and specific procedures that lead to behavioral change;

F. To describe and evaluate the functions and role of the group leader;

G. To have a clear idea of the nature of how the WDEP system works.

H. To compare and contrast reality therapy with some of the other models in the textbook;

I. To critically evaluate the approach, including knowing the advantages and limitations of reality therapy; and

J. To explore applying reality therapy in multicultural settings by looking at the strengths and limitations of using reality therapy with culturally diverse clients.

II. *Key Terms to Identify and Define*
- responsibility
- success identity
- self-evaluation
- choice theory
- behavior evaluation
- total behavior
- cycle of counseling
- replacement program
- "give-up behaviors"
- existential phenomenological
- positive addiction
- involvement
- plan of action
- commitment
- four psychological needs
- "pictures in our heads"
- paradoxical techniques
- quality world
- skillful questioning
- "picture album"

III. *Lecture Outline: Notes and Comments*
   A. Introduction
      1. Compare and contrast reality therapy with the psychoanalytic model and with the experiential approaches.
      2. In what ways does reality therapy share concepts with the cognitive-behavioral approaches?
   B. Key Concepts and the Practice of Reality Therapy in Groups
      1. *Human needs and purposeful behavior.* I suggest a discussion of the four psychological needs (belonging, power, freedom, and fun) from the vantage point of how these needs relate to our behavior. Choice theory is a useful perspective that describes our attempt to satisfy these basic needs.
      2. *Responsibility.* Since this is a core concept in reality therapy, we devote considerable time to discussing how members might either accept or avoid responsibility.
      3. *Existential-phenomenological orientation.* Glasser's approach shares much in common with the existential approach. Reality therapy is based on the assumption that we choose our own goals and are responsible for the kind of world we create for

ourselves. We are not viewed as helpless victims, rather we behave for a purpose and we are able to mold our own destiny. Ask students to discuss the implications of these assumptions as they apply to working with a diverse client population. Students find Glasser's notion of depressing, angering, and headaching to be interesting ideas. For Glasser, we can change these behaviors only when we recognize that what we are doing is the result of our choices.

4. *Total behavior.* Glasser believes that we always have control over what we do and that therefore it is best to focus on what we are doing, rather than how we are feeling. Have students discuss the implications of the focus on doing and thinking as a reference point for group interaction. Do students believe that if they change what they are doing and thinking that their feelings will automatically change?

5. *Value judgments and self-evaluation.* We usually focus on this topic because reality therapy raises the issue of the group leader's encouraging members to make value judgments about their current behavior. We get into discussions on the role of the leader's values and how these values affect the group. This opens up the discussion of imposing versus exposing one's values on the group. It also opens up the topic of possible value clashes with certain types of clients.

6. *Controversial aspects of reality therapy.* This approach is useful in generating discussion of key issues in the therapeutic process such as the rejection of the medical model, playing up the present and playing down the past, deemphasis on transference, and giving little or no attention to unconscious factors. It is interesting to compare reality therapy with psychoanalysis, with focus on the implications for practice of group work with such diverse perspectives.

7. *Role and function of the group leader.* A useful focus of discussion is on the role of the group leader as a teacher. Reality-therapy group leaders are verbally active and directive and they frequently teach members better alternatives. What are the implications of this role for group leaders?

8. *The counseling environment.* Discuss the ways that the group leader's personal involvement with the member is the basic foundation for the practice of effective reality therapy. Explore with students those attitudes and behaviors of the group leader that promote change.

9. *Exploring wants, needs, and perceptions.* In my class, I ask students to generate questions that will help them pinpoint their wants and needs. I then show them how the question "What do you want?" is one of the most important questions that group leaders can raise.

10. *Focus on current behavior.* I discuss with students the implications of reality therapy and its stress on what we are doing

presently. I attempt to show them how the past can be brought into the discussion if it relates to what the member is presently concerned about. We discuss some of the advantages of focusing on current behavior in working with various client populations in groups.
11. *Behavior evaluation.* The core of effective reality therapy consists of getting members to honestly explore the question "Does your present behavior have a reasonable chance of getting you what you want now, and will it take you in the direction you want to go?" We spend time in class on thinking of ways to challenge members to look at what they are doing to determine if this is getting them what they want and need.
12. *Planning and action.* Much of what reality therapists do in their groups is to help members develop an action plan that will lead to changing what they are doing, thinking, and feeling. In my classes, I spend a good bit of time with students on learning how to formulate and implement effective plans. We talk about realistic plans and ways of creating a support system to carry out these plans. We also discuss the importance of getting clients to make a commitment to following through with their plans. I emphasize the importance of developing plans that belong to the members, as opposed to the group leaders deciding upon a plan of action for the members.
13. *Questioning.* How is skillful questioning useful in reality therapy groups? We focus on teaching group leaders to learn *what* questions to ask, *how* to ask them, and when to ask them.

C. Evaluation of Reality Therapy
1. Reality therapy is a good model to contrast with most of the other approaches that have been studied.
2. Ask students to identify what they consider major contributions and limitations of this approach.
3. In working with groups that are characterized by cultural diversity, what are some of the potential strengths and limitations of the practice of reality therapy?

Focus Questions for Chapter 15: Reality Therapy in Groups
1. Discuss the basic assumptions underlying the reality therapy model. Include in this discussion some mention of the key concepts of the approach.
2. What are the main functions of the reality therapy group leader? How might you relate to this role as a leader?
3. Reality therapy focuses on *current behavior.* It tends to downplay feelings, attitudes, one's past, while it focuses on the reality of what one is doing now. What are your thoughts about this approach?

4. According to the reality therapy model, factors such as transference, unconscious motivation, and mental illness are ways to sidetrack reality and responsibility. What are your reactions to this view?

5. How does the following question capture the essence of contemporary reality therapy: *What are you doing?*

6. In what ways is contemporary reality therapy grounded in existential/phenomenological principles? What are the implications for group work?

7. What are the central functions played by the leader in a reality therapy group?

8. What is the essence of choice theory?

9. Explain Glasser's concept of total behavior.

10. Discuss the concept of *responsibility* in the reality therapy model.

11. What role does *involvement* play in the group leader's style? How can the leader demonstrate active involvement?

12. The reality therapy group is based on the assumption that change will take place only if members develop a *plan for change* and stick with the *commitment to change*. What are some ways that you could encourage members to both develop these plans and stick with their commitments?

13. Write a critical evaluation of the reality therapy model of group. Include mention of aspects you might want to include in your own style of group leadership.

Quiz: Comprehension Check
Indicate whether each of the following statements is *T* (true) or *F* (false) as it applies to reality therapy in groups.

(F) 1. Group members should be allowed to talk about past situations in childhood for these experiences shape the person of today.

(F) 2. Reality therapy emphasizes feelings and attitudes, for the assumption is that behavior will not change unless feelings and attitudes change first.

(T) 3. According to Glasser, the way to achieve a successful life is through responsible actions and strength.

(F) 4. Transference must be dealt with fully and resolved if a group member is to make progress.

(F) 5. Reality therapy groups typically begin with an assessment that leads to a diagnostic evaluation of a specific emotional/behavioral disorder.

(T) 6. Group members are expected to make specific plans for responsible behavior, and then to develop a commitment to follow through with these plans.

(T) 7. If members do not complete their contracts, excuses are not accepted.

(T) 8. The role of a group leader includes being a teacher and modeling responsible behavior.
(F) 9. Glasser's current thinking is that it is the reality therapist's role to act as a moralist since he or she is expected to make value judgments about the members' behaviors.
(T) 10. Reality therapy is well suited to brief interventions in crisis-counseling situations.

Quiz: Reality Therapy in Groups

1. According to reality therapy:
   a. insight is essential for change to occur.
   b. people create their own disturbances by accepting irrational beliefs.
   * c. involvement is considered the core of therapy.
   d. self-rating is necessary for mental health.

2. What is the reality therapy view of the medical model?
   a. a useful way to understand psychopathology
   b. a useful tool to make a diagnosis
   c. of value in group with psychotics
   * d. a means of providing excuses to people who are behaving in irresponsible ways

3. The founder of reality therapy is:
   a. Albert Ellis.
   b. Albert Bandura.
   c. Alfred Adler.
   d. Sidney Jourard.
   * e. William Glasser.

4. Which of the following is *not* a key concept of reality therapy?
   a. Members must make commitments.
   * b. Members focus on unconscious motivation.
   c. Members make value judgments of their behavior.
   d. Members focus on the present not the past.

5. Contemporary reality therapy is best captured by the question:
   a. What are you feeling?
   b. What are thinking?
   * c. What are you doing?
   d. What are experiencing?
   e. Both (a) and (b).

6. Which of the following is (are) *not* true of reality therapy?
   a. Leaders do not accept blaming.
   b. Therapists shape behavior through punishment.
   c. Focus is on attitudes and feelings.
   d. Therapy is a didactic process.
   * e. Both (b) and (c)

7. Regarding the role of self-evaluation in the reality therapy group, which is true?
   a. The group leader judges the morality of the actions of members.
   b. The leader teaches members moral behavior in an active way.
   * c. Members must decide for themselves the quality of their actions.
   d. Both (a) and (b).

8. The function of the reality therapy group leader is:
   a. to model responsible behavior for the members.
   b. to question members about what they are doing now.
   c. to encourage members to formulate specific plans for change.
   d. to establish personal involvement with the members.
   * e. all of the above.

9. Which of the following would *not* be a function deemed important by a reality therapy group leader?
   a. setting limits in a group
   b. getting members to evaluate their own behavior
   c. being willing to have his or her own values challenged
   * d. working through transference relationships
   e. exploring and clarifying values

10. Which of the following is an integral part of a reality group?
    * a. contracts
    b. dream work
    c. working on the life scripts of members
    d. reenacting past events in the present
    e. analysis of games

11. According to Glasser, all people have a need for:
    a. striving for superiority.
    * b. fun, freedom, and power.
    c. understanding why they do what they do.
    d. resolving polarities within them.
    e. achieving the goals of their parents.

12. The main task of the reality therapy group leader is:
    a. to confront irrational beliefs.
    b. to become an existential partner with other searching members.
    c. to focus on ways of helping members gain insight into their own current behavior.
    * d. to encourage members to make value judgments regarding their present behavior.

13. Which of the following is *not* a key concept of reality therapy?
    a. responsibility
    b. quality world
    c. human needs
    d. emphasis on the present
    * e. unfinished business

14. Which of the following would *not* be a typical part of the reality therapy group?
    * a. exploring childhood experiences
    b. working on contracts
    c. giving positive feedback
    d. using role-playing procedures
    e. examining current behavior

15. Which method is often used in reality therapy?
    a. behavior-oriented methods
    b. the contract method
    c. use of role playing
    d. confronting clients
    * e. all of the above

16. If members are to make changes, the reality therapist assumes:
    a. that members must develop a plan for change.
    b. that members must be willing to change.
    c. that members must make a commitment to change.
    * d. all of the above.
    e. none of the above.

17. Which is *not* a part of reality therapy groups?
    a. contracts
    b. homework assignments
    * c. dream work
    d. exploring values
    e. confrontation

18. Reality therapy emphasizes:
    * a. responsible planning.
    b. looking at why we think as we do.
    c. gaining insight into the core of a problem.
    d. fully experiencing one's feelings.
    e. both (c) and (d).

19. Contemporary reality therapy is grounded in the principles of:
    a. behavior therapy.
    b. experiential therapy.
    c. object-relations therapy.
    * d. existential/phenomenological orientation.
    e. person-centered orientation.

20. Which of the following is the most recent book by William Glasser?
    a. *Positive Addiction*
    * b. *Choice Theory*
    c. *Reality Therapy*
    d. *The Identity Society*
    e. *Schools without Failure*

CHAPTER 16 COMPARISONS, CONTRASTS, AND INTEGRATION

Focus Questions
1. In considering the diversity of systems of group counseling, do you see any basis for a commonality concerning the goals of group counseling? Explain your view.
2. If you were asked in a job interview how you saw your role as a group counselor, how would you answer?
3. The issue of structuring a group can be discussed from the viewpoint of a continuum ranging from being extremely nondirective to highly directive. Where are you on this continuum? How much structure do you think is optimal for group functioning?
4. What are your views concerning the division of responsibility in a group? How much do you see as the leader's responsibility, and how much is the members' responsibility? How can you avoid the danger of assuming too much or not enough of the responsibility for the direction of the group you are leading? What do you see as the areas for which members are primarily responsible?
5. The various theories of group counseling each generate different techniques. What are some of the techniques that you are most drawn to?
6. When do you think techniques fail? What are some ways that you can increase the chances of techniques serving a useful purpose? What are your guidelines for the effective use of group techniques?
7. If you were asked what model of group you would tend to use, what would you answer? Explain.
8. List a few of the aspects you *most* like from each of the major theoretical approaches to group work. Briefly discuss.
9. After reading the section in the textbook on the applications of the integrated eclectic model, attempt to formulate your own synthesis. How would you tie together several of the theories you have studied? What are the major aspects of your own personal theory of group counseling?
10. Thinking from the perspective of the stages of a group's development, show what concepts you would be most inclined to draw from for each of the various stages. Show specific concepts from the various theories that would help you make sense of group process from the beginning to the end of a group. Can you think of ways to integrate thinking/feeling/behaving perspectives at each of these stages?

CHAPTER 17   THE EVOLUTION OF A GROUP: AN INTEGRATIVE PERSPECTIVE

Focus Questions

1. In this chapter a number of themes are presented with a "typical group" in mind, and then group practitioners with varying orientations work with group members and the themes that emerge. Identify those approaches that are the closest to your thinking and discuss the reasons for your affinity to these approaches.

2. Identify some of the themes that have developed in a group that you have been a member of; then, in a fashion similar to this chapter, take some of the various approaches to group work and show how the different theoretical perspectives apply. How would your group be a different experience depending on the theoretical persuasion of the leader?

3. What are some of the areas of overlap among the various theories you've studied, as these therapies apply to the themes that frequently emerge in a group? Look especially for goals of group, therapeutic procedures, and group techniques.

4. If you were asked to develop your own theory of group work by taking key elements (both concepts and techniques) from each of the approaches you studied, what would your theory look like in outline form?

PART IV

Guidelines for Study and Preparation: Final Examination
and
Take Home Practice Final Examination

What follows is a comprehensive self-test to help students check their comprehension of the material. This Take Home Practice Examination will be most useful in preparing for the in-class final examination.

GUIDELINES FOR STUDY AND PREPARATION:
Final Examination

The final examination is based on the Fifth Edition of *Theory and Practice of Group Counseling* and the *Student Manual*. There are 200 objective-type questions covering all chapters in the above books. Below are a few hints for preparation:

- Take the attached "Take Home Practice Final" which directly follows these guidelines.
- In the *Student Manual* for *TPGC*, at the end of each of the theory chapters is a **Quiz and Comprehension Check** (ten true/false items and ten multiple-choice items). BE SURE TO TAKE THESE COMPREHENSION CHECKS after you've finished studying a theory chapter. Keep up-to-date. These checks will give you an indication of how well you are mastering the material. Review these comprehension checks in preparation for the final exam.
- Take the **Pre-Chapter Self-Inventories** for each of the theory chapters in the *Student Manual for Theory and Practice of Group Counseling*.
- In the *Student Manual* is a **Glossary of Key Terms** for each theory chapter. You should be familiar with these key concepts and terms.
- In the *Student Manual*, each theory chapter has a neat and concise **Stages of Development of Group** (for all ten theories). This is an excellent way to apply each theory to the developmental stages of a group. These summary charts will be a useful tool for review.
- The *Student Manual* has a **Summary of Basic Assumptions and Key Concepts** for each theory chapter. Read these summaries both before you read a chapter, and then again when you've finished the chapter. These summaries—along with the **Evaluations** at the end of each chapter in the *TPGC* textbook—will be invaluable as a study tool and device for review.
- After you've finished reading the theory chapters be sure to take the **Comprehension Check and General Test** in the *Student Manual* (after Chapter 17). See Appendix I for an answer key for the Comprehension Check and General Test. This will be an ideal way to check your overall grasp of the material that will be on the final exam.
- There are **Essay Questions for Review and Study,** after the 150 items on the Comprehension Check and General Test. It would be a great idea to form a small-study group with some friends in this class and go over these questions, and to review the chapter quizzes in the *Student Manual*.
- Review Chapters 16 and 17 on application and integration as a way to help you formulate your own integrative approach.
- Keep up-to-date with your readings, and then schedule an intensive review a couple of weeks prior to the final exam.
- As you study each theory chapter in the *TPGC* textbook, focus on the key concepts of each theory as they apply to group practice.

- In the textbook, become very familiar with the **Role and Functions of the Group Counselor,** from each of the ten theories addressed.
- In the textbook, the chapters end with an **Evaluation of the Approach.** Have a clear idea of the major contributions and strengths of each approach to group, and also the limitations of each approach. Have a grasp of some ways to apply each approach to multicultural populations.

About the Final Examination

The final examination is based on both the textbook and student manual—*Theory and Practice of Group Counseling, Fifth Edition.* There are 200 objective items, divided as follows:

    50 multiple-choice questions from Chapters 1–5
    20 conceptual items (see the Practice Exam for sample items)
    30 multiple-choice items on an overview of all the approaches
    10 multiple-choice items from each of the ten theory chapters

TAKE HOME PRACTICE FINAL EXAMINATION

True-False. For each therapy approach named, decide if the statement is *T* (true) or *F* (false) as it applies to the *particular theory* of group counseling.

The Psychoanalytic Approach to Groups

(F) 1. Transference in the analytic group is viewed as a sign of ineffective work on the therapist's part.

(T) 2. Interpretations are made by both the leader and members.

(T) 3. Countertransferences are feelings of group leaders toward certain members.

(T) 4. Insight is a vital part of the analytic group.

(T) 5. Resistance is considered a critical therapeutic factor that needs to be analyzed and dealt with fully.

(T) 6. Group work entails free association to dreams in the analytic model.

(F) 7. The member makes all interpretations, and the therapist resists any interpretations for the group member.

(T) 8. Working with the past is considered a basic part of group work.

(T) 9. A goal of analytic group work is restructuring of one's personality.

(F) 10. The alternate session, which includes meeting without the group leader, is discouraged as a part of analytic practice.

Adlerian Group Counseling

(F) 11. The Adlerian group puts more focus on unconscious than conscious factors.

(T) 12. Feelings of inferiority are related to one's style of life.

(F) 13. Working with early memories is not a part of the Adlerian group.

(F) 14. The leader's role is to be very nondirective, thus forcing members to find their own structure.

(T) 15. Insight is essential for change in the Adlerian view, thus leaders work toward helping members discover the causes of their problems.

(T) 16. Interpretation is a technique often used in group work.

(T) 17. Adlerian groups stress taking action to change.

(T) 18. A primary role of group leaders is to challenge mistaken beliefs of members.

(T) 19. Focus on birth order and family constellation is a part of group procedures.

(T) 20. Exploration of one's unique lifestyle is a basic procedure in the Adlerian group.

Psychodrama

(F) 21. Fritz Perls is the originator of psychodrama.

(F) 22. Psychodrama focuses on identifying ego status.

(T) 23. Spontaneity and action are central aspects of psychodrama.

(T) 24. Catharsis is a vital part of psychodrama.

(F) 25. Psychodrama is based on a cognitive understanding of the causes of one's difficulties.

(F) 26. The protagonist is the symbolic figure in a member's life that antagonizes the member.

(F) 27. The auxiliary ego is always played by the director.

(T) 28. The magic shop is a technique to clarify values.

(T) 29. Role reversal is a procedure that can enable members to feel empathy for others.

(F) 30. Psychodrama encourages members to talk about their past in an analytic manner, so that they can analyze certain dynamics.

The Existential Approach to Groups

(T) 31. The existential group stresses a personal relationship between members and leader.

(F) 32. The basic goal of group is to uncover unconscious dynamics.

(T) 33. The existential view of death gives meaning to life.

(T) 34. Authenticity is a basic concept in group work.

(F) 35. A basic procedure in group is free association.

(F) 36. Dream work is stressed in the existential group.

(F) 37. Resistance and its analysis is the core of the existential group.

(F) 38. Guilt is seen as neurotic in the existential theory.

(F) 39. Anxiety is something to be eliminated in a successful existential group.

(F) 30. Anxiety is a sign of "inauthentic existence."

The Person-Centered Approach to Groups

(F) 41. The leader's technical skill is considered to be more important than the relationship a leader creates with the members.

(F) 42. Empathy is based on an accurate diagnosis of members' problems.

(F) 43. Techniques and structured exercises are typically used to structure a group experience in this style.

(F) 44. Diagnosis and evaluation are central to person-centered group.

(F) 45. Interpretation is frequently done by the person-centered leader.

(F) 46. Immediacy and congruence are basically the same.

(F) 47. A contract is essential before group work can proceed.

(T) 48. Person-centered groups are basically experiential.

(T) 49. Much research has been carried out in person-centered groups.

(F) 50. Abraham Maslow is the founder of the person-centered approach.

Gestalt Therapy

(F) 51. In Gestalt dream work, the leader interprets the underlying meaning of dreams.

(F) 52. Gestalt theory is basically an insight therapy.

(F) 53. A basic goal of the Gestalt group is to resolve the transference neurosis.

(T) 54. Nonverbal cues are stressed in the Gestalt group.

(T) 55. Gestalt is a here-and-now type of therapy.

(T) 56. Unfinished business is given emphasis in group.

(F) 57. Gestalt group stresses cognitive restructuring and cognitive awareness of origins of problems.

(F) 58. The mirror technique is considered a basic Gestalt procedure.

(F) 59. The use of auxiliary egos is a common procedure in Gestalt group.

(F) 50. In Gestalt therapy awareness is best described as analytic introspection and insight.

Transactional Analysis

(F) 61. In TA group work emphasis is placed on understanding and resolving transference relationships.

(F) 62. A racket is a life script that develops from the Adult ego state.

(T) 63. A basic premise of TA is that what has been decided in childhood can be redecided in adulthood.

(F) 64. Injunctions are defined as a collection of "bad feelings" that one stores up to justify actions called for in the life script.

(T) 65. TA stresses cognitive aspects and action.

(F) 66. The "Critical Parent" is a basic part of the Adult ego state.

(F) 67. Since people are "scripted" during childhood, they do not make basic decisions at this time.

(T) 68. Contracts are seen as an essential part of a group.

(F) 69. The process by which people become aware of their Parent, Adult, and Child ego states is known as functional analysis.

(T) 70. Messages that come from the Parent ego state of the parents are known as counterinjunctions.

Behavioral Group Therapy

(T) 71. In behavioral groups, assessment and treatment proceed simultaneously.

(T) 72. The newer thinking in the behavioral approach emphasizes cognitive and social factors.

(T) 73. Techniques must be demonstrated for effectiveness and they must fit the treatment plan.

(F) 74. If people expect to change, they must explore the roots of a particular problem.

(T) 75. Cognitive restructuring is often used in the behavioral group.

(F) 76. A goal of behavioral groups is to tap unconscious processes and integrate polarities.

(F) 77. Role playing is generally *not* a part of the behavioral group.

(T) 78. Setting up a hierarchy is a procedure used in assertion training groups.

(F) 79. Developing baseline data is a procedure used at the final stages of a group.

(T) 80. A primary concern of the final stages of group is promoting the transfer of learning.

Rational Emotive Behavior Therapy

(F) 81. REBT is basically an experiential approach.

(T) 82. REBT is basically a didactic and education method.

(T) 83. According to Ellis, we become emotionally disturbed because we indoctrinate ourselves with faulty ideas.

(T) 84. Traumatic situations are not the cause of emotional disturbance; rather, it is one's beliefs about these situations that cause problems.

(T) 85. Group members are expected to confront and attack the faulty thinking of other members.

(F) 86. Transference and its resolution is seen as a basic procedure in REBT groups.

(F) 87. In REBT, role-playing is designed to elicit strong, repressed feelings.

(F) 88. A basic job of REBT leaders is to assist members in reliving past experiences as though they were happening here and now.

(T) 89. Homework is assigned in the group.

(T) 90. REBT is essentially a behavioral approach.

Reality Therapy in Groups

(F) 91. Reality therapy holds that it is essential to change attitudes *before* behaviors can change.

(F) 92. Reality therapy leaders make value judgments for the members.

(T) 93. Total behavior is a key concept in reality therapy.

(F) 94. According to Glasser, all people have a need to strive for superiority.

(F) 95. Reality therapy stresses looking at why we do what we do.

(T) 96. Confrontation is a basic procedure in group.

(T) 97. Contracts are often a part of the group process in reality therapy.

(T) 98. If members are to change, they must make a commitment to change.

(F) 99. Dreams are typically explored in the reality therapy groups.

(T) 100. The focus of group work is on current behavior.

Conceptual Items. In each of the following numbered items, four of the five conceptual items listed are a series of concepts or therapeutic techniques related to *one particular* group model. One item does not relate to the same model. Indicate which work or phrase does not belong in the series.

Example: (a) analysis of resistance, (b) free association, (c) assertion training, (d) dream analysis, (e) interpretation of transference. (The item that does not fit is (c) assertion training, which is a technique in behavioral group. The other four items are techniques in a psychoanalytic group.)

A   101.   (a) style of life, (b) irrational beliefs, (c) self-rating, (d) counter-propaganda, (e) rational philosophy of life

A   102.   (a) earliest memories, (b) irrational beliefs, (c) self-rating, (d) counter-propaganda, (e) rational philosophy of life

E   103.   (a) family constellation, (b) birth order, (c) social determinants of personality, (d) basic mistakes, (e) ABC theory of personality

B   104.   (a) unconditional positive regard, (b) unfinished business, (c) empathy, (d) active listening, (e) congruence

E   105.   (a) stroking, (b) scripts, (c) ego states, (d) rackets, (e) dream work

B   106.   (a) cognitive restructuring, (b) script analysis, (c) thought stopping, (d) relaxation training, (e) stress inoculation

A   107.   (a) exaggeration technique, (b) mirror technique, (c) magic shop, (d) double technique, (e) future projection

E   108.   (a) rackets, (b) injunctions, (c) games, (d) early decisions, (e) the soliloquy technique

B   109.   (a) protagonist, (b) contingency contracting, (c) auxiliary ego, (d) acting out conflicts, (e) role playing

B   110.   (a) freedom and responsibility, (b) determinism, (c) self-awareness, (d) anxiety, (e) meaning

C   111.   (a) internal dialogue, (b) rehearsal technique, (c) implosion therapy, (d) empty-chair technique, (e) making the rounds

C   112.   (a) free association, (b) analysis of dreams, (c) script analysis, (d) analysis of resistance, (e) analysis of transference

E   113.   (a) transference, (b) countertransference, (c) resistance, (d) unconscious dynamics, (e) ego states

D   114.   (a) quality world, (b) self-evaluation, (c) commitment, (d) reliving past experiences in the here and now, (e) current behavior

D   115.   (a) confronting irrational beliefs, (b) ABC theory, (c) homework assignments, (d) working through transference relationships, (e) empirical method

C   116.   (a) responsible planning, (b) contract method, (c) exploring childhood memories, (d) examining current behavior, (e) making value judgments

E   117.   (a) here-and-now focus, (b) awareness, (c) figure formation, (d) unfinished business, (e) interpretation of transference

B 118. (a) reversal technique, (b) stress inoculation, (c) exaggeration techniques, (d) rehearsal technique, (e) making the rounds

B 119. (a) a cognitive approach, (b) a psychodynamic approach, (c) an action-oriented approach, (d) a learning approach, (e) a systematic approach

C 120. (a) focus on specific behavior, (b) developing a treatment plan, (c) exploration of unconscious dynamics, (d) action-oriented methods, (e) evaluation and assessment

E 121. (a) a didactic approach, (b) a form of cognitive-behavior modification, (c) an insight-oriented therapy, (d) a highly directive approach, (e) an experiential form of therapy

B 122. (a) self-instruction, (b) empty-chair technique, (c) self-reinforcement, (d) thought stopping, (e) self-directed changes

D 123. (a) catharsis, (b) insight, (c) reliving earlier experiences, (d) focus on current behavior, (e) spontaneity and creativity

E 124. (a) guilt, (b) anxiety, (c) aloneness, (d) death and meaning, (e) unconscious determinism

C 125. (a) modeling, (b) behavior rehearsal, (c) mirror technique, (d) coaching, (e) reinforcement procedures

Matching Exercises. On the left side are names of key figures associated with a particular group approach. Match the person named to the therapy approach with which he is associated.

C	126.	J. L. Moreno	(a)	reality therapy
E	127.	Robert Goulding	(b)	Adlerian therapy
B	128.	Rudolf Dreikurs	(c)	psychodrama
A	129.	William Glasser	(d)	existential
D	130.	Rollo May	(e)	transactional analysis

On the left side are techniques associated with a particular group approach. Match the technique to the approach.

D	131.	report of earliest recollections	(a)	psychoanalytic group
E	132.	magic shop	(b)	Gestalt group
B	133.	reversal technique	(c)	TA group
C	134.	script analysis	(d)	Adlerian group
A	135.	analysis of transference	(e)	psychodrama

On the left side are some key concepts associated with a particular approach. Match the concepts to the approach.

D	136.	accurate empathy	(a)	rational emotive behavior therapy
E	137.	cognitive restructuring	(b)	psychodrama
B	138.	catharsis and insight	(c)	reality therapy
A	139.	ABC theory	(d)	person-centered approach
C	140.	choice theory	(e)	behavioral approach

Again, match the left and right sides.

D	141.	freedom and responsibility	(a)	psychoanalytic
A	142.	insight and working through	(b)	behavioral
E	143.	unfinished business	(c)	TA
C	144.	decisions and redecisions	(d)	existential
B	145.	empirical validation of results	(e)	Gestalt

Match the left and right column.

D	146.	an educational model	(a)	psychodrama
A	147.	an experiential model	(b)	psychoanalytic
B	148.	an insight approach	(c)	reality therapy
E	149.	a relationship-oriented approach	(d)	rational emotive behavior therapy
C	150.	choice theory	(e)	person-centered approach

Multiple-Choice Items: Be sure to answer each of the questions in this section within the theoretical framework of the following specific categories. For ease of taking the test in this section, test items have been clustered into five items per theory. Select the *one best* answer that fits with the perspective under consideration.

The Psychoanalytic Approach to Groups

151. In a group setting, free association could be used for:
    a. uncovering repressed material.
    b. encouraging spontaneity among members.
    c. working on dreams in the group.
    d. interacting with one another in the group.
*   e. all of the above.

152. Interpretations in the analytic group are made by:
    a. the group leader.
    b. the member who is working on a problem.
    c. by all the members at times.
    * d. all of the above.

153. An advantage of a group is that:
    a. multiple transferences can be formed.
    b. the group becomes a family of yesterday.
    c. members can benefit from one another's work.
    d. members can identify their own transferences.
    * e. all of the above.

154. The goal of the analytic group is to work toward:
    a. adequate social adjustment.
    b. a restructuring of one's personality.
    c. achieving intense feelings in the here and now.
    * d. both (b) and (c).

155. The final stage of the analytic group consists of:
    a. analysis of transference.
    b. working through dreams.
    * c. conscious personal action and social integration.
    d. understanding all of the causes of one's behavior.
    e. both (a) and (b).

Adlerian Group Counseling

156. According to Adler, feelings of inferiority:
    a. are a neurotic manifestation.
    b. hamper one's creativity.
    * c. are related to power.
    d. both (a) and (b).
    e. none of the above.

157. Which of the following is *not* a basic characteristic of Adlerian groups?
    a. establishing a therapeutic relationship
    b. analysis of individual dynamics
    c. insight
    * d. developing rapport in a group through sharing of dreams
    e. a reorientation

158. Goal alignment refers to the state whereby:
    a. all the members develop common goals.
    * b. both the leader's and the members' goals are the same.
    c. members actually carry out new behavior beyond the group session.
    d. members accept the goals of society by adjusting to the dominant norms.

159. The Adlerian view of insight is:
    a. personality is not changed unless there is insight.

b. insight is necessary as a requisite for personality change to occur.
* c. insight is understanding translated into constructive action.
d. insight always follows a release of intense feelings.
e. insight is a cognitive understanding of one's behavior and the specific origins of personality and behavioral problems.

160. The primary goal of the Adlerian group leader is:
a. interpreting resistance.
b. uncovering repressed material.
* c. to challenge the beliefs and goals of the members.
d. to develop a treatment plan and evaluate results.
e. both (a) and (b).

Psychodrama

161. The psychodrama method emphasizes:
* a. spontaneity and creativity.
b. an intellectual understanding of the causes of conflicts.
c. a way of challenging irrational beliefs.
d. understanding of life scripts.
e. all of the above.

162. The role of the psychodrama group leader is:
a. to be a producer.
b. to be a catalyst/facilitator.
c. to be an observer/analyzer.
* d. all of the above.
e. none of the above.

163. The protagonist is:
* a. the person selected to work.
b. the symbolic figure in a member's life that antagonizes the member.
c. the group member who serves as an alter-ego.
d. both (b) and (c).

164. The purpose of this technique is to assist members in clarifying their values.
a. the mirror technique
* b. the magic shop
c. doubling
d. future projection
e. the soliloquy

165. The third phase of a psychodrama consists of:
* a. sharing what was observed and personal reactions during the action phase.
b. encouraging the protagonist to act out a conflict.
c. the leader giving an interpretation of the dynamics of behavior.
d. some type of nonverbal behavior.

The Existential Approach to Groups

166. The existential group focuses on:
   * a. here-and-now forces within the group.
   b. unresolved conflicts that have been repressed in childhood.
   c. techniques designed to assist members in gaining catharsis.
   d. both (b) and (c).

167. The existential view of death is:
   a. that it renders us hopeless.
   b. that it gives life less meaning.
   * c. that it gives meaning to every moment.
   d. that it creates an existential vacuum.

168. The function of the existential group leader is:
   a. to understand the member's subjective world.
   b. to explore the member's past history.
   c. to challenge each member to discover alternatives.
   * d. both (a) and (c).

169. According to existentialists, the central issue in therapy is:
   a. resistance.
   * b. freedom and responsibility.
   c. transference.
   d. experiencing feelings.
   e. none of the above.

170. In the existential group, the leader would tend to:
   * a. challenge the members to become aware of their choices.
   b. draw upon dramatic and cathartic techniques.
   c. aim for a catharsis.
   d. urge members to get rid of guilt and anxiety.
   e. encourage a regression into one's early past.

The Person-Centered Approach to Groups

171. A person-centered group leader is best described as a:
   a. teacher.
   b. friend.
   c. judge.
   * d. facilitator.
   e. expert.

172. Which of the following is considered important in this approach?
   a. accurate interpretation on the leader's part
   b. accurate diagnosis and formulation of a treatment plan
   * c. the attitudes of the leader
   d. analysis of underlying dynamics
   e. none of the above

173. The *congruence* of the group leader implies:
   a. empathy.

      b. respect.
      c. immediacy.
*   d. genuineness.
      e. unconditional positive regard.

174. Immediacy refers to:
      a. helping members get concrete.
      b. the authenticity of the leader.
      c. the capacity of the leader to attain accurate empathy.
*   d. dealing with what is happening in the here and now of a relationship.
      e. getting clients to see how their past is connected to immediate problems.

175. The crucial factor that determines the outcome of the person-centered group is:
      a. the leader's technical skills.
*   b. the leader's relationship with the members of the group.
      c. the leader's knowledge of group dynamics.
      d. the member's willingness to think rationally.
      e. defining specific and measurable goals.

Gestalt Therapy

176. A basic goal of the Gestalt therapy group is:
      a. to uncover repressed childhood experiences.
      b. to challenge one's philosophy of life.
*   c. to deal with whatever becomes figural for the client.
      d. to resolve transference neurosis.
      e. all of the above.

177. Gestalt therapy focuses on:
      a. exploration of the past.
*   b. the here and now.
      c. the future.
      d. both the past and the future.
      e. whatever time period the client wants to explore.

178. In Gestalt therapy, awareness is best described as:
      a. introspection.
      b. insight.
*   c. recognition of current feelings, actions, and sensations.
      d. recognition of why one struggles with certain problems.
      e. none of the above.

179. Which technique encourages participants to give expression to one side of themselves that they rarely express?
*   a. the reversal technique
      b. the exaggeration technique
      c. the go-around technique

    d. implosive therapy
    e. none of the above

180. Gestalt experiments are aimed at:
    a. teaching members how to think rationally.
* b. integrating conflicting sides within a member.
    c. teaching clients how to discover causes of future problems.
    d. helping members understand unconscious dynamics.
    e. both (c) and (d).

Transactional Analysis

181. Collections of bad feelings that people use to justify their life script are known as:
    a. basic decisions.
* b. rackets.
    c. games.
    d. counter-injunctions.
    e. none of the above.

182. According to the Gouldings, people:
    a. are victims of the messages given to them by their parents.
    b. are scripted in a passive way.
* c. have a role in accepting certain messages as children.
    d. have very few real choices since injunctions determine their behavior.

183. The Gouldings stress which of the following in their group practice?
    a. life scripts
* b. redecision
    c. analysis of early childhood fixations
    d. transference
    e. none of the above

184. According to TA, a contract by group members:
    a. should be decided by the leader.
    b. once decided should not be revised.
    c. is an essential place to begin a group.
    d. can be made in steps and is subject to change.
* e. both (c) and (d).

185. The practice of TA in groups:
    a. must be done in a strict TA style.
    b. can be incorporated with Gestalt.
    c. can be incorporated with behavioral techniques.
    d. begins with a detailed case history of each member.
* e. both (b) and (c).

Behavioral Group Therapy

186. In a behaviorally-oriented group, the decision to use certain techniques to change behavior is based on:

a. the group leader's therapeutic style.
   b. the desires of the members.
* c. the demonstrated effectiveness of the technique.
   d. the theoretical view of the leader.
   e. none of the above.

187. Which of the following is *not* considered a behavioral technique?
   a. self-instruction
* b. the empty chair technique
   c. cognitive restructuring
   d. self-reinforcement
   e. thought stopping

188. Which of the following would be a part of the early stages of behavior groups?
   a. building of cohesiveness
   b. identifying problematic behavior
   c. assessment
   d. developing baseline data
* e. all of the above

189. A primary concern during the final stages of the behavior group is:
* a. promoting transfer of learning.
   b. developing a therapeutic contract.
   c. role-playing various situations.
   d. establishing baseline data.
   e. providing relaxation training methods.

190. Which type of group best describes behavioral methods applied to helping people overcome stress reactions in specific situations?
* a. stress inoculation training
   b. assertion training groups
   c. behavioral groups for self-directed change
   d. problem-solving groups
   e. none of the above

Rational Emotive Behavior Therapy

191. REBT in groups can best be characterized as:
   a. an experiential approach.
   b. a phenomenological approach.
* c. a cognitive approach.
   d. a psychodynamic adaptation.

192. In REBT groups, homework assignments are:
   a. carried out in the group.
   b. carried out in daily life.
   c. seen as a basic part of the REBT method.
   d. ways of practicing new behavior.
* e. all of the above.

193. Marathon groups are:
    a. rarely used in REBT.
    b. seen as counterproductive for cognitive work to occur.
    * c. often used in conjunction with weekly REBT groups.
    d. designed primarily to elicit feelings.
    e. both (a) and (b).

194. The role of the REBT group leader is best seen as:
    * a. a teacher.
    b. a facilitator of feelings.
    c. an I-Thou model of relating.
    d. a blank screen that receives projections.
    e. a moralist.

195. In REBT, role-playing:
    a. is rarely done.
    b. is of a strictly cognitive nature.
    c. is designed to evoke strong feelings.
    * d. involves a cognitive-emotive evaluation of feelings and beliefs.

Reality Therapy in Groups

196. Which of the following is *not* a key concept of reality therapy?
    a. members must make commitments
    * b. members focus on unconscious motivation
    c. members evaluate their behavior
    d. members focus on the present, not the past

197. Which of the following is an integral part of reality groups?
    * a. making an evaluation of one's total behavior
    b. dream work
    c. working with life scripts
    d. re-living past events in the present

198. Which of the following is *not* a key concept of reality therapy?
    a. total behavior
    b. quality world
    c. human needs
    d. choice theory
    * e. unfinished business

199. Which of the following is *not* typical of reality groups?
    a. working on contracts
    b. giving positive feedback
    c. using role playing
    * d. exploring childhood experiences
    e. examining current behavior

200. The main task of the reality therapist group leader is:
    a. to confront irrational ideas.
    b. to merely listen and reflect.

* c. to encourage members to evaluate their behavior.
  d. to teach members the right way to live.
  e. to experience feelings.

PART V
Final Examination for Theory and Practice of Group Counseling

The Final Examination for Theory and Practice of Group Counseling is a comprehensive coverage of both the textbook and student manual. Following the exam itself is an answer key.

FINAL EXAMINATION FOR THEORY AND PRACTICE OF GROUP COUNSELING

Directions: The first part of this test covers group process concepts and issues based on Chapters 1–5 (Basic Elements of Group Process) of *Theory and Practice of Group Counseling* (Fifth Edition, 2000). The second part of the test covers the theories of group counseling based on Chapters 6–15 of *TPGC*). Be sure and record the number of your test on the SCAN TRON and RETURN THE TEST **UNMARKED** with your answer sheet. On the multiple-choice items, your task is to select the *one best* answer among the listed alternatives.

Introduction to Group Work (#1–10)

1. A major difference between group therapy and group counseling lies in:
   a. the techniques used to facilitate group process.
   b. the group process and stages of group.
   c. the goals for the group.
   d. the age of the participants.

2. All of the following are true of structured groups *except:*
   a. they are designed to impart information.
   b. they aim at teaching people how to solve problems.
   c. they have the purpose of helping people learn how to create their own support systems outside of the group.
   d. they tend to be long-term groups.

3. All of the following are common denominators between self-help groups and therapy groups *except:*
   a. both are led by qualified professionals.
   b. both types of groups encourage suppport and stress the value of affiliation.
   c. both kinds of groups aim for behavioral change.
   d. both make use of the group process.

4. Which type of group focuses on remediation, treatment, and personality reconstruction?
   a. support groups
   b. therapy groups
   c. self-help groups
   d. psychoeducation groups
   e. task groups

5. If you are involved in group work with culturally diverse populations, it will be important for you to:
   a. be an expert in each of the populations.
   b. accept the challenge of modifying your strategies to meet the unique needs of the members.

c. be of the same ethnic background as the members in your group.
d. conduct empirical research on your groups to validate your effectiveness.

6. Which of the following is/are an advantage/advantages of group work with multicultural populations?
    a. Members can gain much from the power and strength of collective group feedback.
    b. Modeling operates in groups.
    c. In groups, people learn that they are not alone in their struggles.
    d. Cross-cultural universality often exists in such groups.
    e. All of the above.

7. Which of the following groups is designed to assist committees, planning groups, community organizations, discussion groups, study circles, and learning groups to correct or develop their functioning?
    a. task groups
    b. self-help groups
    c. psychotherapy groups
    d. psychoeducation groups
    e. counseling groups

8. Assume you are leading a group and a particular ethnic client tends to be very quiet. Which of the following might best explain this silence?
    a. This is surely a sign of a resistant client.
    b. This is evidence that this client does not want to be in the group.
    c. The silence may indicate politeness and a sense of respect.
    d. This hesitation is best interpreted as a stubborn refusal to be open.
    e. This member should be asked to leave the group.

9. If you are intending to form a group composed of culturally diverse members, it would be important for you to:
    a. prepare the clients for the group experience.
    b. have an unstructured group.
    c. develop specific goals for each member.
    d. expect a high level of resistance from the members.
    e. screen out any potential members who are not highly verbal.

10. Which approach is grounded on the premise that basic human dimensions are important regardless of culture?
    a. the provincial perspective
    b. the narrow approach to multiculturalism
    c. the collaborative approach
    d. the universal or transcultural perspective
    e. the culture-specific perspective

Overview of Group Leadership Skills (#11–17)
Select the one term or phrase that best completes the description:

11. Opening up clear and direct communication among members; helping members to assume increasing responsibility for the group's direction
    a. suggesting
    b. facilitating
    c. goal setting
    d. giving feedback
    e. none of the above

12. Offering possible explanations for certain thoughts, feelings, and patterns of behavior
    a. interpreting
    b. evaluating
    c. giving feedback
    d. active listening
    e. all of the above

13. Challenging participants to look at discrepancies between their words and actions or body messages and verbal communication; pointing to conflicting information or messages
    a. interpreting
    b. questioning
    c. confronting
    d. suggesting
    e. initiating

14. To prepare members to assimilate, integrate, and apply in-group learning to everyday life
    a. modeling
    b. suggesting
    c. interpreting
    d. initiating
    e. terminating

15. Grasping the essence of a message at both the feeling and the thinking levels in order to help members sort out conflicting feelings and thoughts
    a. clarifying
    b. interpreting
    c. evaluating
    d. suggesting
    e. none of the above

16. Identifying with members by asssuming their internal perspective so as to foster trust and to encourage deeper levels of self-exploration
    a. questioning
    b. empathizing

    c. reflecting feelings
    d. giving feedback
    e. summarizing
17. Offering information to help members develop alternative courses of thinking and action
    a. giving feedback
    b. suggesting
    c. interpreting
    d. supporting
    e. terminating

Ethical Issues in Group Practice (#18–27)

18. Which of the following captures the essence of informed consent?
    a. having members sign a contract before joining a group
    b. telling members in some detail about the nature and purpose of the group
    c. having members decide upon all of the activities of the group
    d. making sure that groups will always be composed of voluntary membership.

19. On the matter of coercion and pressure in a group, members should know that:
    a. some pressure is to be expected as a part of group process.
    b. they have a right to be protected against undue pressure.
    c. coercion to make acceptable decisions may be a part of group procedure.
    d. they may well be pressured to participate in threatening nonverbal exercises.
    e. both (a) and (b)

20. On the issue of psychological risks in groups, what can be safely said?
    a. In a well-designed group, there are really no psychological risks.
    b. Since groups can be catalysts for change, they also contain risks.
    c. Members can be given guarantees that a group will not involve risks.
    d. There are risks only when members are not properly screened.

21. Which of the following would *not* be considered one of a group member's rights?
    a. the right to expect protection from verbal or physical assaults
    b. the right to expect complete confidentiality
    c. the right to know the leader's qualifications
    d. the right to help from the group leader in developing personal goals
    e. the right to expect freedom from undue group pressure

22. Confidentiality in groups is:
    a. a legal right of every member.
    b. something that members can be guaranteed.
    c. limited by state laws.

d. an absolute that can never be broken for any reason.
e. granted to all participants and the leader automatically under the privilege communication ruling.

23. Regarding the issue of freedom of exit, which is the recommended course of action?
    a. Members should be able to leave at any time they wish without any explanation.
    b. Members should never be allowed to leave a group once they begin for any reason.
    c. Members who are thinking of leaving should bring the issue up for discussion in the session.
    d. Members can leave a group if they experience discomfort with conflict that occurs in the group.

24. The ACA Code of Ethics specifically prohibits:
    a. any form of dual relationships.
    b. sexual relationships between counselor and client.
    c. any kind of friendship or social relationship with former clients.
    d. the use of nonverbal interactive exercises.
    e. a group leader's disclosure about his or her values.

25. Which of the following is probably the most controversial ethical issue in the preparation of group workers?
    a. combining of experiential and didactic training methods
    b. expecting students to formulate their own theoretical perspective
    c. the theoretical orientation of the person doing the training
    d. expecting trainees to be aware of their own personal issues that might detract from their effectiveness as leaders
    e. teaching of group leadership skills

26. When making difficult ethical decisions as a group leader, it is helpful to:
    a. know the ethical code of your professional organization.
    b. consult with colleagues.
    c. get supervision and training during the early stages of your development as a leader.
    d. base your practice on sound, informed, and responsible judgment.
    e. all of the above

27. Regarding the matter of imposing leader values on members:
    a. group leaders might expose (but not impose) their values when appropriate.
    b. it is best for leaders to keep their values private whenever they have a conflict with members.
    c. group leaders should always share their values if members ask.
    d. group leaders cannot avoid imposing their values on members.

The Stages of Development of a Group (#28–30)

28. Inclusion and identity are the primary tasks of which stage of a group?
    a. initial stage
    b. transition stage
    c. working stage
    d. final stage

29. Which stage is generally characterized by increased anxiety and defensiveness?
    a. initial stage
    b. transition stage
    c. working stage
    d. final stage

30. Which is the correct sequence of the stages of a group?
    a. transition, initial, working, consolidtion
    b. initial, transition, consolidation, working
    c. initial, transition, working, consolidation
    d. transition, initial, consolidation, working

Initial Stage of a Group (#31–35)

31. During a group's initial phase, members can best build trust by:
    a. waiting until someone takes the first risk and then opening up.
    b. revealing their lack of trust.
    c. relying on "trust exercises" initiated by the leader (i.e., falling backward and trusting others to catch you).
    d. sharing non-intimate details about themselves.
    e. waiting until they feel comfortable before sharing inner struggles and fears.

32. When group members receive painful feedback from other members, they should be encouraged to:
    a. listen carefully to what they are being told and explore how what they are hearing fits for them.
    b. accept what they are being told as valid.
    c. consider leaving the group.
    d. leave the group and return when they feel better.
    e. confront the person who is giving the feedback.

33. During the early stages of a group the central process involves:
    a. testing and confronting the leader.
    b. sharing of leadership functions by the members.
    c. orientation and exploration.
    d. a willingness to share threatening material.
    e. none of the above.

34. The foundation of the group is:
    a. the development of trust.
    b. the development of group cohesion.

c. the development of group norms.
   d. the working-through of transference feelings.
   e. learning to stay in the here and now.

35. The ACA's ethical standard pertaining to screening group members states that:
    a. counselors screen prospective group counseling participants and select members whose needs and goals are compatible with the goals of the group.
    b. leaders screen members only if their theory calls for screening.
    c. screening is not consistent with the democratic ideal.
    d. screening is appropriate only for psychotherapy groups.

Transition Stage of a Group (#36–40)

36. Group behaviors such as competition, rivalry, and challenges to the leadership are indicative of:
    a. transference.
    b. lack of trust.
    c. struggle for control.
    d. none of the above.

37. During which phase are group leaders most often confronted personally and professionally?
    a. initial
    b. early
    c. transition
    d. working
    e. final

38. Which of the following statements illustrates an ineffective confrontation?
    a. "You are a phony! You are always smiling and that's not real."
    b. "I feel uncomfortable with you because I'm afraid of what you think of me."
    c. "I find it very difficult to be open with you."
    d. "I don't like it that I often feel inadequate when I am with you."
    e. "Many of the things you say really hurt me."

39. When a member is consistently silent during group sessions, it is best to:
    a. consistently call on that person.
    b. invite them to explore what their silence means.
    c. avoid attacking them for their silences.
    d. engage in harsh confrontation to get them to participate.
    e. (b) and (c)

40. Who is the author of *Theory and Practice of Group Counseling* (Fifth Edition, 2000)?
    a. Alfred Adler
    b. James Robert Bitter

c. Marianne Schneider Corey
d. Gerald Corey
e. Irvin Yalom

Working Stage and Final Stage of a Group (#41–50)

41. A group in the working stage is characterized by:
    a. the members' commitment to explore significant problems.
    b. tentativeness.
    c. the assuming of greater responsibility by the leaders.
    d. all of the above.

42. Which of the following is *not* usually a characteristic of the working stage?
    a. group cohesion
    b. universality (ability to see commonalities of life issues)
    c. relatively few interpersonal conflicts and struggles
    d. less dependence on the leader for direction
    e. development of a healing capacity within the group

43. All of the following are characteristic of a nonworking group except:
    a. members or leaders use power and control over others.
    b. members are interested in themselves and others.
    c. conformity is prized.
    d. the group relies heavily on cathartic experiences without seeking to understand them.
    e. norms are not clear.

44. The therapeutic factor that operates in group when members believe that change is possible is known as:
    a. acceptance.
    b. hope.
    c. catharsis.
    d. cohesion.
    e. none of the above.

45. The therapeutic factor in groups that involves affirming a person's right to have his or her feelings and values is:
    a. caring.
    b. acceptance.
    c. empathy.
    d. intimacy.
    e. feedback.

46. The therapeutic factor in groups by which members let each other know how they are affected by their behavior in group is:
    a. feedback.
    b. empathy.
    c. acceptance.
    d. intimacy.
    e. caring.

47. Which of the following therapeutic factors in groups is the means by which open communication occurs within the group?
    a. humor
    b. emapthy
    c. caring
    d. the cognitive component
    e. self-disclosure

48. All of the following are considered to be therapeutic factors of a group *except:*
    a. freedom to experiment.
    b. commitment to change.
    c. cognitive restructuring.
    d. confrontation.
    e. resistance.

49. During the final stage of a group, which of the following is *not* the functions of members at this time?
    a. dealing with their feelings about separation and termination
    b. developing ground rules and setting of group norms
    c. evaluating the impact the group has had on them
    d. preparing for generalizing their learning to everyday situations
    d. completing any unfinished business within the group
    e. providing others in the group with feedback

50. In helping group members deal with their feelings of separation, it is important for the leader to:
    a. remind them that they can create meaningful relationships outside the group setting.
    b. facilitate open discussion of feelings of loss and sadness.
    c. be able to deal with his or her own feelings about the termination of the group.
    d. all of the above.
    e. none of the above.

Conceptual Items (#51–70)
The following items present a series of related concepts or techniques pertaining to one therapeutic approach. One of the items in each series does not fit with the other four items. Select the one word or phrase that does *not* fit in each series.

51. (a) soliloquy, (b) double technique, (c) stress inoculation, (d) mirror technique, (e) magic shop

52. (a) unconditional positive regard, (b) private logic, (c) congruence, (d) internal locus of evaluation, (e) empathy

53. (a) life scripts, (b) injunctions and early decisions, (c) rackets, (d) strokes, (e) early memories

54. (a) choice theory, (b) ABC theory, (c) irrational beliefs, (d) musturbatory philosophy, (e) rational philosophy of life

55. (a) lifestyle assessment, (b) working with transference and countertransference, (c) the alternate session, (d) insight and working through, (e) dream analysis

56. (a) total behavior, (b) WDEP system, (c) redecisional therapy, (d) choice theory, (e) identifying wants, needs, and perceptions

57. (a) unfinished business, (b) the figure-formation process, (c) contact and resistance to contact, (d) BASIC ID, (e) energy and blocks to energy

58. (a) ego states, (b) social skills training, (c) cognitive restructuring, (d) modeling, (e) social learning theory

59. (a) total behavior, (b) teleology, (c) creativity and choice, (d) inferiority/superiority, (e) Individual Psychology

60. (a) coping-skills techniques, (b) the buddy system, (c) life-script analysis, (d) problem solving, (e) coaching

61. (a) search for meaning, (b) freedom and responsibility, (c) injunctions and early decisions, (d) search for authenticity, (e) self-awareness

62. (a) exploring wants, needs, and perceptions, (b) exploration of unconscious experiences, (c) evaluating current behavior, (d) commitment to an action plan, (e) avoiding excuses and blaming

63. (a) catharsis, (b) spontaneity and creativity, (c) encounter and tele, (d) surplus reality, (e) stress inoculation training

64. (a) social interest, (b) lifestyle, (c) basic mistakes, (d) working with polarities, (e) early recollections

65. (a) insight, (b) reinforcement, (c) contingency contracts, (d) behavior rehearsal, (e) problem solving

66. (a) transactional analysis, (b) dream analysis, (c) game analysis, (d) structural analysis, (e) script analysis

67. (a) cognitive restructuring, (b) making the rounds, (c) fantasy approaches, (d) exaggeration exercises, (e) reversal techniques

68. (a) behavioral assessment, (b) precise therapeutic goals, (c) treatment plan, (d) objective evaluation, (e) exploring the individual's dynamics

69. (a) exploration of resistance, (b) free association, (c) exploring multiple transferences, (d) exploring one's position in the family constellation, (e) looking for connections between the present and the past.

70. (a) behavioral assessment, (b) establishing and maintaining the relationship, (c) exploring the individual's dynamics, (d) insight, (e) reorientation

Multiple-Choice (#71–100)
Overview of Various Approaches to Group

71. Erik Erikson's theory is:
    a. a developmental model.
    b. based on the psychosexual developmental stages, but extends these stages.
    c. basically a psychosocial model.
    d. a model based on critical turning points at the various stages of life.
    e. all of the above.

72. Which approach would be least interested in exploring early childhood experiences?
    a. psychoanalytic
    b. Gestalt therapy
    c. reality therapy
    d. existential therapy
    e. Adlerian

73. Concepts of fictional finalism, basic mistakes, and social interest are a part of which theory?
    a. TA
    b. Adlerian
    c. reality
    d. cognitive-behavioral
    e. existential

74. The process of skillful questioning would most likely be used by a group leader with what orientation?
    a. Gestalt therapy
    b. psychodrama
    c. person-centered therapy
    d. reality therapy
    e. none of the above

75. Unfinished business and avoidance are key concepts of:
    a. behavior therapy
    b. REBT
    c. TA
    d. Gestalt therapy
    e. person-centered therapy

76. Bion's method of interpretation of group process is most closely associated with which approach?
    a. psychodrama
    b. rational emotive behavior therapy
    c. Adlerian therapy
    d. TA
    e. none of the above

77. The object-relations theory is associated with:
    a. Adlerian therapy
    b. psychoanalytic therapy
    c. behavioral therapy
    d. TA
    e. REBT

78. Insight is stressed by which theory?
    a. reality therapy
    b. TA
    c. behavior therapy
    d. psychodrama
    e. none of the above

79. Of the following, which approach would most likely aim to re-create the original family, so that members could work through their unresolved problems?
    a. behavioral
    b. psychoanalytic
    c. TA
    d. existential
    e. person-centered

80. Multimodal group therapy is most closely associated with:
    a. Adlerian therapy
    b. REBT
    c. reality therapy
    d. Gestalt therapy
    e. behavior therapy

81. Identifying and working with ego states would occur in what type of group?
    a. Gestalt
    b. TA
    c. Adlerian
    d. psychodrama
    e. none of the above

82. A group leader with what theoretical orientation would be the least interested in providing structure for the members?
    a. REBT
    b. behavior therapy
    c. person-centered therapy
    d. TA
    e. Adlerian

83. The most significant developments in understanding and dealing with borderline and narcissistic personality disorders have occurred within which theory?
    a. TA

b. reality therapy
  c. existential approach
  d. psychoanalytic therapy
  e. none of the above

84. Which of the following theories would focus mostly on cognition?
   a. Gestalt
   b. Adlerian
   c. reality therapy
   d. behavior therapy
   e. psychoanalytic therapy

85. A group leader with what orientation would be most interested in energy and blocks to energy?
   a. REBT
   b. psychoanalytic
   c. person-centered
   d. Gestalt
   e. Adlerian

86. Shame-attacking exercises are likely to be used in which type of group?
   a. person-centered
   b. reality therapy
   c. behavior therapy
   d. TA
   e. rational emotive behavior therapy

87. Bob and Mary Goulding are associated with which therapeutic approach?
   a. psychodrama
   b. TA
   c. Gestalt therapy
   d. Adlerian therapy
   e. stress-inoculation training

88. Erv and Miriam Polster are associated with which therapeutic approach?
   a. psychodrama
   b. TA
   c. Gestalt therapy
   d. Adlerian therapy
   e. stress-inoculation training

89. Meichenbaum is associated with which therapeutic approach?
   a. psychodrama
   b. TA
   c. Gestalt therapy
   d. Adlerian therapy
   e. stress-inoculation training

90. Moreno is associated with which therapeutic approach?
    a. psychodrama
    b. TA
    c. Gestalt therapy
    d. Adlerian therapy
    e. stress-inoculation training

91. Arnold Lazarus is associated with which therapeutic approach?
    a. reality therapy
    b. TA
    c. multimodal therapy
    d. Adlerian therapy
    e. stress-inoculation training

92. Rudolf Dreikurs is associated with which therapeutic approach?
    a. reality therapy
    b. TA
    c. multimodal therapy
    d. Adlerian therapy
    e. stress-inoculation training

93. A group counselor who would invite a member to "become each part of his or her dream" is most likely working within the framework of:
    a. Jungian therapy.
    b. psychoanalysis.
    c. Adlerian therapy.
    d. Gestalt therapy.
    e. reality therapy.

94. A group counselor who tells the members that the sharing of their dreams, fantasies, and free associations are essential to the work of the group process would most likely be working within the framework of:
    a. Jungian therapy.
    b. psychoanalysis.
    c. Adlerian therapy.
    d. Gestalt therapy.
    e. reality therapy.

95. The technique that consists of bringing an anticipated event into the present and acting out that event is known as:
    a. magic shop.
    b. rehearsal.
    c. experimenting with dialogues.
    d. future projection.
    e. paradoxical procedure.

96. *Insight* and *working through* are procedures that would be most likely used in which type of group?
    a. REBT
    b. psychoanalytic

c. reality therapy
d. TA
e. both (c) and (d)

97. Which theoretical orientation deals with the following five major channels of resistance?
    a. psychoanlytic
    b. Adlerian
    c. Gestalt
    d. psychodrama
    e. TA

98. The term or phrase that best describes a group leader who is behaving in a *congruent* manner is:
    a. unconditional positive regard.
    b. realness or genuineness.
    c. empathic.
    d. countertransference reaction.
    e. immediacy and presence.

99. The group therapist's leadership style that could be characterized by "objectivity, warm detachment, and relative anonymity" is probably operating within the framework of which theoretical orientation?
    a. psychoanalytic
    b. reality therapy
    c. existential therapy
    d. psychodrama
    e. cognitive-behavior therapy

100. A group leader with which theoretical orientation(s) is (are) most likely to structure a group by asking the members to develop contracts?
    a. psychoanalytic therapy
    b. person-centered therapy
    c. TA
    d. behavior therapy
    e. both (c) and (d)

Psychoanalytic Approach To Groups (#101–110)

101. The goal of the analytic group is to work toward:
    a. adequate social adjustment.
    b. bringing about social and political change.
    c. replacing faulty cognitions with functional thoughts.
    d. an emotional catharsis.
    e. a restructuring of one's personality.

102. The psychoanalytic concept that refers to repetition of interpretations and overcoming of resistance, which allows the client to resolve dysfunctional patterns that originated in childhood and to make choices based on new insights, is known as:

a. repetition compulsion.
   b. life script awareness.
   c. working through.
   d. the therapeutic impasse.
   e. countertransference.

103. Which of the statements is true as it relates to the analytic view of the past?
   a. Early learning is irreversible.
   b. Present events are the focus, yet they are connected with the past by asking the client to relate present feelings with past ones.
   c. Analytic group therapists dwell on the past to the exclusion of present concerns.
   d. Analytic group work does not attend to the historical basis of current behavior.
   e. The focus of analytic group work is here-and-now experiencing and staying in the moment.

104. Regarding the concept of the unconscious, all of the following statements are true *except:*
   a. unconscious experiences have a powerful impact on our daily functioning.
   b. consciousness is only a small part of the human experience.
   c. most of human behavior is motivated by forces outside of conscious experience.
   d. painful experiences during early childhood and feelings associated with them are buried in the unconscious.
   e. psychoanalytic group work consists exclusively of exploring past events.

105. An advantage of a group is that:
   a. multiple transferences can be formed.
   b. the group becomes a family of yesterday.
   c. members can benefit from one another's work.
   d. members can learn to identify their own transferences.
   e. all of the above.

106. Insight and the process of working through are considered:
   a. unessential in group work.
   b. necessary before members can be considered ready to leave the group.
   c. necessary for the therapist, but not for the members.
   d. to be things that are accomplished only after a person leaves the group.
   e. essential only for more advanced members.

107. When members meet for a session without a formal leader, this is known in analytic circles as:
   a. the member-oriented session.
   b. the alternate session.

c. organized resistance.
d. self-motivated interation session.
e. none of the above.

108. Which function is generally *not* carried out by an analytic group leader?
    a. pointing out evidence of resistance
    b. relinquishing leadership by encouraging members to interact with one another
    c. making interpretations
    d. demanding contracts from each member as a prerequisite to joining the group
    e. asking questions

109. The final stage of the analytic group consists of:
    a. analysis of transference.
    b. interpretation of resistance.
    c. working through that results in increased consciousness and integration of self.
    d. developing of a sense of cohesion.

110. Which one of the following is *not* a trend or a future direction of psychodynamic group therapy?
    a. The emphasis on treatment is shifting from the "classical" interest in curing neurotic disorders to dealing with personality disorders, such as borderline and narcissistic personality problems.
    b. There is increased attention on establishing a good therapeutic alliance early in the course of therapy.
    c. There is a renewed interest in developing briefer forms of treatment.
    d. Psychodynamic group therapy has greatly declined in popularity.
    e. Time-limited group therapy will be receiving increasing attention in the future.

The Adlerian Approach to Group (#111-120)

111. A major difference between Freud and Adler was that:
    a. Adler was a politically- and socially-oriented psychiatrist who showed concern with the common person.
    b. Adler had no interest in early childhood experiences.
    c. Adler completely rejected the notion of unconscious motivation.
    d. Adler believed that sexual repression caused neurotic disorders.
    e. Adler believed that we are the victims of fate.

112. According to Adler, feelings of inferiority:
    a. are the wellsprings of creativity.
    b. lead to the development of a unique lifestyle.
    c. ultimately lead us to strive for mastery and perfection.
    d. result in attempts to compensate by finding ways in which to control the forces in our lives.
    e. all of the above.

113. Which of the following is *not* a basic characteristic of the Adlerian approach to group work?
   a. establishing a therapeutic relationship
   b. analysis of individual dynamics
   c. awareness and insight
   d. developing rapport in a group through sharing of dreams
   e. reorientation (seeing new alternatives and making new choices)

114. In Adlerian group work, analysis and assessment:
   a. are ways of exploring an individual's dynamics.
   b. are basic to exploring an invdividual's dynamics.
   c. are considered as detrimental to group process.
   d. are seen as neither necessary nor desirable.
   e. are done during the final stage of the group.

115. What best describes the Adlerian view of the therapeutic relationship?
   a. The therapist is considered the expert.
   b. The therapist is expected to maintain distance and objectivity as a way to foster transference.
   c. The therapist is best viewed as a behavioral engineer.
   d. The therapeutic relationship is one between equals.
   e. The therapist should be a friend to the client.

116. "The Question" is a technique used to:
   a. uncover the client's dysfunctional thought patterns.
   b. uncover early childhood trauma.
   c. get clients thinking about future directions.
   d. determine whether an illness is due to organic or psychological factors.
   e. identify transference patterns between group members.

117. The primary role of the Adlerian group counselor is:
   a. interpreting resistances.
   b. uncovering repressed material.
   c. to challenge the beliefs and goals of the members.
   d. to develop a treatment plan and evaluate results.
   e. to devise emotive role-playing situations.

118. Analysis and assessment rely heavily on exploration of the client's:
   a. unconscious motivations.
   b. patterns of resistance displayed in a group.
   c. values.
   d. multiple transferences that become evident in a group.
   e. family constellation, birth order, and early recollections.

119. Which of the following is *not* true of the Adlerian perspective on insight?
   a. Insight is a step toward change.
   b. Insight is a means toward the end of change.

c. People can make abrupt and significant changes without much insight.
   d. Insight can be considered as understanding translated into constructive action.
   e. Insight is a necessary prerequisite for change.

120. Who is the person who translated Adler's concepts into practical applications for group therapy?
   a. Rudolf Dreikurs
   b. James Robert Bitter
   c. Monford Sonstegard
   d. Harold Mosak
   e. none of the above

Psychodrama (#121-130)

121. Which of the following is *not* considered a key concept of psychodrama?
   a. creativity and spontaneity
   b. encounter and tele
   c. dealing with the present
   d. catharsis and insight
   e. social interest and community feeling

122. How is catharsis a part of psychodrama?
   a. Pent-up feelings are released through acting.
   b. Catharisis is not seen as necessary or desirable.
   c. Catharisis is facilitated by the use of certain techniques designed to intensify feelings.
   d. Catharsis is useful only after members fully understand what is causing a particular problem.
   e. both (a) and (c)

123. Which is *not* generally a function of the psychodrama director?
   a. To warm up the group before action takes place.
   b. To coach other members to act as doubles.
   c. To offer suggestions regarding what scenes might be enacted.
   d. To conduct a lifestyle assessment on the members prior to admitting them to a group.
   e. To lead a sharing session after an action segment.

124. Which of the following is *not* considered a technique used in psychodrama?
   a. future projection
   b. exploration of games and life scripts
   c. doubling
   d. the magic shop
   e. role reversal

125. The technique whereby a protagonist speaks directly to the audience by expressing some uncensored feeling or thought is:
    a. the mirror technique.
    b. projection.
    c. soliloquy.
    d. role reversal.
    e. replay.

126. The third phase of a psychodrama consists of:
    a. sharing what was observed during the action period.
    b. encouraging a protagonist to act out a conflict.
    c. the leader's giving an interpretation of the dynamics of behavior.
    d. some type of nonverbal exercise.

127. A special characteristic of psychodrama methods is that they are applicable to:
    a. many other theoretical orientations.
    b. no other theoretical framework.
    c. experiential therapies only.
    d. cognitive and behavioral therapies only.

128. The ventilation of stored-up feelings is known as:
    a. breaking out.
    b. breaking down.
    c. working through.
    d. catharsis.
    e. acting out.

129. Which of the following is (are) an ethical issue(s) in the practice of psychodrama?
    a. the irresponsible use of psychodramatic procedures
    b. untrained persons using psychodramatic approaches
    c. leaders being attracted to psychodrama to fill their own egotistical needs
    d. romanticizing psychodrama as a single approach
    e. all of the above

130. A psychodrama director may say, "That didn't work well enough. May I please do it over?" This is an example of the technique of:
    a. role training
    b. role reversal
    c. doubling
    d. mirroring
    e. replay

The Existential Approach (#131-140)

131. The existential approach is largely:
    a. cognitive therapy.
    b. an experiential therapy.
    c. a relationship-oriented approach.

    d. a psychodynamic approach.
    e. both (b) and (c)

132. The basic goal of the existential group is:
    a. to adjust the members to the demands of society.
    b. to expand self-awareness.
    c. to help members accept the responsibility of choosing.
    d. to treat symptoms so that members call be free of existential anxiety
    e. both (b) and (c)

133. The existential group focuses on:
    a. here-and-now forces within the group.
    b. unresolved conflicts that have been repressed in childhood.
    c. techniques designed to facilitate catharsis.
    d. measuring observable outcomes of a group.
    e. cognitive restructuring.

134. The implication of self-awareness for group practice is that:
    a. repression is a strong factor in human behavior.
    b. humans tend to shy away from awareness of themselves.
    c. awareness of the causes of one's problems provides the key to resolving these problems.
    d. through self-awareness members are confronted with the responsibility to direct their own lives.
    e. through self-awareness members will discover that they have a fixed destiny.

135. The existential view of death is that:
    a. it renders us as hopeless.
    b. it makes life less meaningful.
    c. it gives meaning to every moment.
    d. it creates an existential vacuum.

136. According to the existential viewpoint:
    a. meaning is automatically given to us by the fact that we are humans.
    b. we must create our own meaning in life.
    c. the group leader needs to point out what the meaning of one's life should be.
    d. there is no real meaning to life as the world is meaningless.
    e. none of the above.

137. Authenticity consists of:
    a. making the right choices.
    b. living by the expectations of significant others.
    c. choosing in the face of uncertainty.
    d. taking the stand to define and affirm ourselves.
    e. both (c) and (d)

138. The central issue(s) in therapy, according to the existential view, is (are):
    a. resistance.

b. freedom and responsibility.
   c. transference.
   d. experiencing feelings.
   e. none of the above.

139. The role of techniques in the existential group is that:
   a. techniques should be secondary to understanding members.
   b. techniques can be borrowed from many approaches.
   c. techniques interfere with the therapeutic process.
   d. techniques imply a loss of faith in the client's ability to find his own way.
   e. both (a) and (b)

140. In an existential group, the leader would tend to:
   a. challenge members to become aware of their freedom and responsibility.
   b. draw upon highly dramatic group techniques.
   c. aim for a catharsis for each group member.
   d. urge members to get rid of guilt and anxiety.
   e. encourage a regression to one's early childhood.

Person-Centered Approach to Groups (#141-150)

141. The basic goal of the person-centered group is:
   a. to provide a climate of safety and freedom.
   b. to provide opportunities for multiple transferences.
   c. to provide for ways to bring about cognitive restructuring.
   d. to provide a re-educational experience that tends to increase members' community feeling and social interest.
   e. to assist members in identifying and sharing early recollections.

142. Which of the following is considered important in the person-centered approach?
   a. accurate interpretation on the leader's part
   b. accurate diagnosis and formulation of a treatment plan
   c. the attitudes of the group leader
   d. analysis of underlying dynamics of behavior
   e. none of the above

143. The crucial factor that determines the outcomes of person-centered groups is:
   a. the leader's technical skills.
   b. the leader's relationship with members in the group.
   c. the leader's knowledge of group theory.
   d. the willingness of members to think critically and rationally.
   e. defining specific and measurable goals.

144. The term that best captures the role and function of a person-centered group counselor is:
   a. teacher.
   b. facilitator.

c. expert.
d. director.
e. coach.

145. Rogers described the following pattern of behavior as the first to emerge in a person-centered group:
    a. expression of immediate interpersonal feelings in the group
    b. expression of negative feelings
    c. milling around
    d. description of past feelings
    e. expression of feelings of closeness

146. A limitation of the person-centered approach is:
    a. a lack of research conducted on key concepts.
    b. a tendency for practitioners to give support without challenging clients enough.
    c. the lack of attention to the therapeutic relationship.
    d. the failure to allow clients to choose for themselves.
    e. the lacking of any applicability in working with culturally diverse client groups.

147. What is the value placed by Rogers on research on group process?
    a. It is seen as largely irrelevant.
    b. It is seen as something that should be done exclusively with objective measurement.
    c. It is seen as a process that taps the subjective experience members' views of the group.
    d. It is discouraged because it views members from an external perspective.

148. The attitudes of leader congruence, accurate empathic understanding and unpossessive caring are considered by the person-centered approach to be:
    a. necessary but not sufficient to effect change.
    b. neither necessary nor sufficient factors to effect client change.
    c. both necessary and sufficient factors to effect change within the members.

149. Which of the following is *not* considered a key concept of the person-centered approach?
    a. total behavior
    b. congruence
    c. unconditional positive regard
    d. empathic understanding
    e. personal power

150. Which of the following would the person-centered group leader be least inclined to use?
    a. sharing of personal experiences
    b. using techniques to initiate action

c. reflecting and clarifying
d. listening in an active and sensitive way
e. affirming a client's capacity for self-determination

Gestalt Therapy in Groups (#151-160)

151. Biesser's paradoxical theory of change holds that personal change tends to occur when we:
    a. make resolutions to make specific behavioral changes.
    b. are willing to formulate a contract that identifies what we will do to bring about change.
    c. become aware of what we are as opposed to trying to become what we are not.
    d. act in opposite ways of what we say we want.
    e. strive to act in ways that are expected of us.

152. There are a number of basic principles that underlie the theory of Gestalt therapy. Which of the following is *not* considered one of these principles?
    a. holism
    b. total behavior
    c. field theory
    d. the figure-formation process
    e. organismic self-regulation

153. Of the following, which individual goal would least likely be characteristic of a Gestalt group?
    a. integrating polarities within oneself
    b. achieving contact with self and others
    c. being willing to learn about oneself by engaging in creative experiments
    d. defining one's boundaries with clarity
    e. challenging irrational beliefs

154. The primary function of the Gestalt leader is to:
    a. make interpretation for the members.
    b. serve as a blank screen to foster transference.
    c. suggest experiments that will lead to increased awareness and to heightening of experiencing.
    d. confront clients' basic mistakes, faulty logic, and cognitive distortions.
    e. connect the meanings of dreams to present struggles.

155. The Gestalt group leader:
    a. is mainly a nondirective facilitator.
    b. pays attention to whatever seems to be emerging in moment-to-moment experiencing.
    c. pays attention mainly to a member's belief system.
    d. pays attention to why a person feels a certain way.
    e. remains anonymous so as to foster transference.

156. Unfinished business is related to:
    a. feelings of resentment and guilt.
    b. the fear of dealing with the future.
    c. issues from the past that interfere with present functioning.
    d. the failure to acquire social skills.
    e. both (a) and (c)

157. In Gestalt therapy awareness is best described as:
    a. introspection.
    b. insight.
    c. recognition of current feelings, thoughts, actions, and sensations.
    d. recognition of why one struggles with a certain problem.
    e. none of the above.

158. How is the past dealt with in a Gestalt group?
    a. The past is not considered crucial and is therefore not explored.
    b. Members talk about past experiences and get feedback.
    c. Members attempt to figure out the origin of their problems by recalling early experiences.
    d. The past is brought into the present moment by asking the member to re-experience a past issue as though it were occuring now.
    e. The past is always related to the future.

159. The Gestalt approach to dreams:
    a. asks members to discover the meaning a dream has for them.
    b. teaches members the universal meaning of dream symbols.
    c. rests mainly on the skill of the leader in interpreting the dream for a member.
    d. always involves the use of free association.
    e. looks for connections to past traumatic events.

160. Which technique encourages participants to give expression to a side of themselves they rarely express?
    a. the reversal technique
    b. paradoxical intention
    c. systematic desensitization
    d. the mirror technique
    e. doubling

Transactional Analysis in Groups (#161-170)

161. Which ego state is the "processor of information?"
    a. parent
    b. adult
    c. child

162. Eric Berne's position was that people were:
    a. scripted by their parents.
    b. to a large degree victims of their injunctions and of the decisions based on them.
    c. primarily free to make new decisions.

d. determined by genetic influences.
   e. both (a) and (b)

163. Which of the following comes closest to Berne's view?
   a. People behave in situations by responding to a stimulus.
   b. People are motivated primarily by striving for social interest.
   c. People are shaped from their first few years by a script that they follow during the rest of their life.
   d. People are socialized by cultural values.
   e. People are mainly motivated by attempting to overcome feelings of inferiority.

164. A familiar emotion, learned and encouraged in childhood and experienced in many different stress situations, and a collection of bad feelings that people use to justify their life scripts are known as:
   a. basic decisions.
   b. rackets.
   c. games.
   d. counterinjunctions.
   e. basic psychological life positions.

165. According to Mary and Robert Goulding, people:
   a. are victims of the messages given to them by their parents.
   b. are scripted in a passive way.
   c. have a role in accepting certain messages as children.
   d. have very few real choices.
   e. both (a) and (b)

166. The Gouldings stress which of the following in their practice of group therapy?
   a. life scripts
   b. redecisions
   c. analysis of early childhood fixations
   d. transference
   e. lifestyle assessment

167. An ongoing series of transactions that ends with a negative payoff, which advances feeling badly and which is called for by the script is the definition of:
   a. rackets.
   b. games.
   c. early decisions.
   d. scripts.
   e. strokes.

168. The practice of TA in groups:
   a. must be done in a puristic and strictly TA style.
   b. can be incorporated with techniques from Gestalt therapy and behavioral techniques.
   c. begins with an analysis of each participant's family constellation.

    d. begins with a detailed case history of each member.
    e. is based on the assumption that the group leader eventually becomes a transference object.

169. Transactional analysis is best suited for:
    a. individual counseling.
    b. group counseling.
    c. work with regressed psychotics.
    d. work only with highly functioning people.
    e. individuals with borderline personality disorders

170. One of the advantages of using a TA group with multicultural populations is:
    a. the focus on the authority of the group leader as expert.
    b. the experiential nature of TA techniques.
    c. the use of a contract.
    d. the unstructured nature of a TA group.
    e. the use of highly emotional role-playing techniques.

Behavior Therapy in Groups (#171-180)

171. What technique spells out the behaviors to be performed, changed, or discontinued, as well as the rewards associated with the achievement of these goals?
    a. reinforcement
    b. modeling
    c. contingency contracts
    d. behavioral rehearsal
    e. coaching

172. Which is (are) true of the application of behavioral techniques in a group?
    a. These techniques remain under continual evaluation.
    b. They are experiential in nature.
    c. They are designed to produce insight.
    d. They are usually aimed at catharsis.
    e. all of the above

173. If people want and expect change, the behavioral group leader contends that it is important that:
    a. they explore the past roots of a particular problem.
    b. they gain insight into the causes of a problem.
    c. they engage in detailed introspection.
    d. they take specific actions to effect change.
    e. all of the above.

174. Which of the following statements is *false* as applied to behavior therapy in groups?
    a. Behavioral techniques can be incorporated into the humanistic therapies in a systematic way.
    b. Behavioral procedures can be a part of an eclectic framework.

c. Behavioral techniques are typically tools used by the leader to assist participants to work toward their self-determined goals.
   d. Behavioral techniques are designed to elicit catharsis followed by insight.
   e. Behavioral procedures are a part of the treatment plan.

175. Which of the following is *not* a behavioral technique?
   a. contingency contracts
   b. the reversal experiment
   c. modeling
   d. relaxation training
   e. behavior rehearsal

176. Which of the following would be characteristic of the initial stages of the behavior therapy group?
   a. The members would be given very little structure so that they might create their own group.
   b. Members would be given information concerning how a group functions.
   c. A treatment contract would be developed.
   d. Experiential exercises would be used to facilitate interaction and to create trust.
   e. Both (b) and (c).

177. Which of the following is generally a part of the working phase of the behavioral group?
   a. reinforcement
   b. behavioral rehearsal
   c. cognitive restructuring
   d. the buddy system
   e. all of the above

178. A primary concern during the final stages of the behavioral group is:
   a. promoting transfer of learning.
   b. developing a therapeutic contract.
   c. role-playing various situations.
   d. establishing baseline data
   e. providing relaxation-training methods

179. Which of the following techniques is generally *not* associated with the assertion training group?
   a. cognitive restructuring
   b. life script questionnaire
   c. coaching
   d. reinforcement
   e. homework

180. The process of identifying and evaluating one's cognitions, understanding the negative impact of thinking on behavior, and learning more appropriate self-messages is known as:
    a. stress-inoculation training.
    b. cognitive restructuring.
    c. behavioral rehearsal.
    d. behavioral alignment.
    e. problem solving.

Rational Emotive Behavior Therapy in Groups (#181-190)

181. According to REBT, people develop psychological disturbances because of:
    a. a traumatic event.
    b. failure to receive love from significant others.
    c. their belief about certain events.
    d. unfinished business from their past.
    e. playing out of their life script.

182. Which of the following would have the least applicability to a REBT group?
    a. unconditional acceptance
    b. role-playing
    c. feedback
    d. interpretation of early memories
    e. reinforcement and penalties

183. REBT employs what kind of method(s) to help members resolve their personal problems?
    a. cognitive methods
    b. behavioral methods
    c. emotive methods
    d. all of the above
    e. only (a) and (b)

184. Which one of the following methods would a REBT group therapist be least likely to employ?
    a. analysis of basic psychological life positions
    b. cognitive homework
    c. shame-attacking exercises
    d. use of humor
    e. psychoeducational methods

185. A REBT group leader is interested in:
    a. creating a climate in a group where members can reenact unfinished business from their past.
    b. showing members how they have created their own misery.
    c. helping members resolve transference relationships within the group.

d. assisting members to fully experience whatever they are feeling in the present moment.
   e. completing a lifestyle assessment as a basis for progressing in group work.

186. In REBT role-playing
   a. is rarely done, as it needlessly stirs up emotion.
   b. is limited strictly to cognitive aspects.
   c. is designed to evoke intense feelings.
   d. involves a cognitive-emotive evaluation of feelings and beliefs.
   e. involves a member acting out all the various roles of a present conflict.

187. REBT belongs to which general category of theory?
   a. psychodynamic
   b. client-centered and experientially oriented
   c. existential
   d. cognitive-behavior-action oriented
   e. relationship oriented

188. According to REBT, change will come about:
   a. mainly through a commitment to consistently practice new behaviors that challenge old and ineffective ones.
   b. only when we discover the source of our problems.
   c. generally after we relive a traumatic situation in therapy and work through the impasse that prevents new growth.
   d. by awareness itself.
   e. when significant others give us what we expect from them.

189. The group leader is likely to begin a group by:
   a. asking the members to complete the life-script checklist.
   b. using nonverbal exercises to build trust.
   c. teaching members the basics of the ABC theory.
   d. using direct and confrontive techniques to undermine the members' irrational thinking.
   e. creating a climate of warmth and empathy.

190. REBT group practitioners may ask members to imagine some of the worst things they can think of and then to train themselves to develop appropriate emotions in the place of disruptive ones. This is an example of which technique?
   a. systematic desensitization
   b. teaching the ABC's
   c. rational emotive imagery
   d. teaching coping self-statements
   e. psychoeducational methods

Reality Therapy in Groups (#191-200)

191. Which of the following is (are) emphasized by reality therapy group leaders?
    a. focusing on actions and thoughts
    b. focusing on insight into causes of one's problems
    c. changing attitudes, which will eventually lead to behavioral change
    d. exploring feelings as a way to release unexpressed emotions
    e. reliving childhood experiences in the present moment

192. Contemporary reality therapy is best captured by which question?
    a. What are you feeling?
    b. What are you thinking?
    c. What are you doing?
    d. What are you experiencing?
    e. What is your body telling you?

193. Which of the following is true of reality therapy?
    a. Leaders encourage members to blame their current situation on negative influences from their past.
    b. Therapists shape behavior through punishment.
    c. Leaders have the role of making an evaluation of each member's present behavior.
    d. Members identify their wants and needs, assess the direction of their behavior, and make plans for change.
    e. Members learn the necessity of expressing feelings associated with painful events.

194. Regarding the role of self-evaluation in the reality therapy group, which is true?
    a. The group leader evaluates the member's current behavior.
    b. The leader teaches moral behavior in an active way.
    c. Members are expected to evaluate the quality of their actions and decide if they want to change.
    d. Other group members decide for a given individual if his or her behavior is effective.

195. Which of the following would *not* be a function deemed important by a reality therapy group leader?
    a. setting limits in a group
    b. getting members to evaluate their own behavior
    c. being willing to have his or her own values challenged
    d. working through transference relationships
    e. exploring and clarifying values

196. In a reality therapy group, what are the procedures that lead to change?
    a. the WDEP system
    b. carrying out shame-attacking exercises
    c. participating in role-playing

    d. the group leader selecting techniques that have been empirically tested as proven to be effective in bringing about change
    e. dealing with one's family of origin as it unfolds in the here-and-now context of the group situation

197. Which of the following is *not* a key concept of reality therapy?
    a. an existential/phenomenological orientation
    b. choice theory
    c. purposeful behavior
    d. total behavior
    e. basic psychological life positions

198. What is the view of the reality therapist on transference?
    a. A group is an ideal place to work out transference distortions.
    b. Transference is not a significant factor in group work.
    c. Transference is the result of inept leadership.
    d. A disadvantage of groups is that they foster transferences not only with the leader but with other members.

199. All of the following are key procedures that are often used in a reality therapy group except:
    a. exploring wants, needs, and perceptions.
    b. getting members to determine if what they are currently doing is leading them in the direction they want to go.
    c. self-evaluation.
    d. planning and action.
    e. using criticism as a way to encourage change.

200. What is the theory underlying the practice of reality therapy?
    a. holistic theory
    b. choice theory
    c. social learning theory
    d. behavioral theory
    e. humanistic theory

APPENDIX I
Answer Key to Final Examination for Theory and Practice of Group Counseling

1. c	41. a	81. b	121. e	161. b
2. d	42. c	82. c	122. e	162. e
3. a	43. b	83. d	123. d	163. c
4. b	44. b	84. b	124. b	164. b
5. b	45. b	85. d	125. c	165. c
6. e	46. a	86. e	126. a	166. b
7. a	47. e	87. b	127. a	167. b
8. c	48. e	88. c	128. d	168. b
9. a	49. b	89. e	129. e	169. b
10. d	50. d	90. a	130. e	170. c
11. b	51. c	91. c	131. e	171. c
12. a	52. b	92. d	132. e	172. a
13. c	53. e	93. d	133. a	173. d
14. e	54. a	94. b	134. d	174. d
15. a	55. a	95. d	135. c	175. b
16. b	56. c	96. b	136. b	176. e
17. b	57. d	97. c	137. e	177. e
18. b	58. a	98. b	138. b	178. a
19. e	59. a	99. a	139. e	179. b
20. b	60. c	100. e	140. a	180. b
21. b	61. c	101. e	141. a	181. c
22. c	62. b	102. c	142. c	182. d
23. c	63. e	103. b	143. b	183. d
24. b	64. d	104. e	144. b	184. a
25. a	65. a	105. e	145. c	185. b
26. e	66. b	106. b	146. b	186. d
27. a	67. a	107. b	147. c	187. d
28. a	68. e	108. d	148. c	188. a
29. b	69. d	109. c	149. a	189. c
30. c	70. a	110. d	150. b	190. c
31. b	71. e	111. a	151. c	191. a
32. a	72. c	112. e	152. b	192. c
33. c	73. b	113. d	153. e	193. d
34. a	74. d	114. a	154. c	194. c
35. a	75. d	115. d	155. b	195. d
36. c	76. e	116. d	156. e	196. a
37. c	77. b	117. c	157. c	197. e
38. a	78. d	118. e	158. d	198. b
39. e	79. b	119. e	159. a	199. e
40. d	80. e	120. a	160. a	200. b

APPENDIX II
InfoTrac Flow Chart

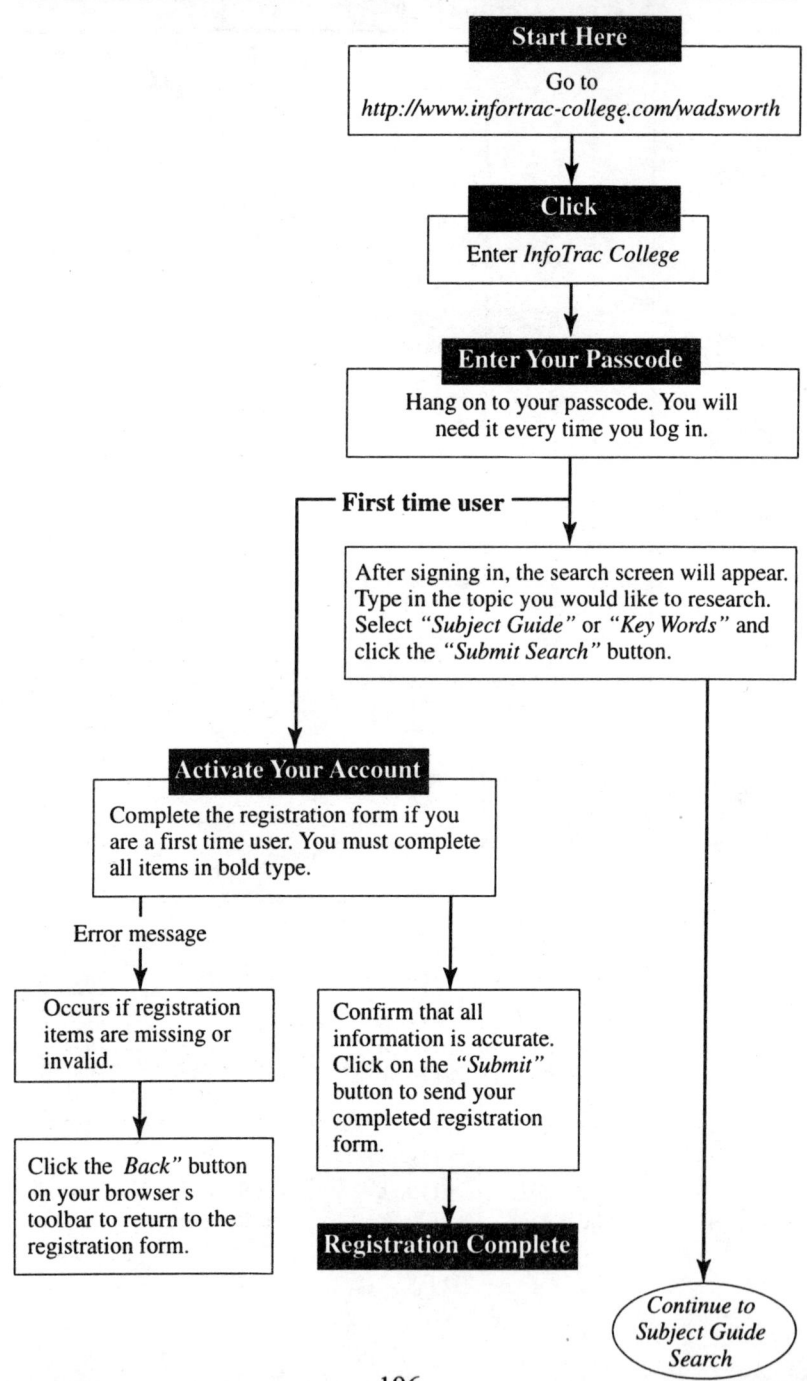

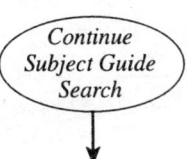

Continue Subject Guide Search

Your marked articles will have the bibliographic information at the top of the article followed by an abstract (when available) and the full text of the article. To browse through your articles, click on the *"Previous"* or *"Next"* button.

Using PowerTrac

With **PowerTrac**, a more complex search can be conducted. Click on the *"Down Arrow"* on the *"Select an Index"* listbox, choose the criteria you want to use. The code for your criteria will appear in the entry box. Type your criteria in the entry box after the code.

If you want to search by multiple criterion, simply repeat the process with an operator between them.

- *Logical operators* (and/or/not) specify inclusive or exclusive relationships between search terms or result sets.

- *Proximity operators* (Wn, Nn) specify that two search terms must be within a specified distance (in words) of each other. Proximity operators work only with free text indexes such as keywords, abstracts, text and titles.

- *Range operators* (since, before, etc.) specify upper bounds, lower bounds or both in searches for numeric data. Numeric indexes include publication dates, number of employees and annual sales.

- *Nesting operators* determine the order in which operators are evaluated.

End